D0290581

ROBIN KIMBALL EISENBEIS

A

GIFT

FOR

LIFE

Skills Everyone
Needs to Win

Here's what folks have to say about A Gift for Life...

A must read for anyone "building your life resume"!
Jesse Itzler
Co-Founder Marquis Jet, partner in Zico coconut water and an owner of NBA's Atlanta Hawks

A Gift for Life takes a personal look at our world, guiding us on the process of evaluating relationships, money, and dreams through life lessons and experiences. Robin explains the importance of caring about people on a personal level no matter how small. Explaining finances in a way that someone with no understanding of savings can learn massive life lessons. Telling of vision, dreams, and adventure from her own experiences and why you should be just as daring in life. The traits and lessons Robin emphasizes are things every young adult should be taught and value!
Ben Hatfield
1st Lieutenant, United States Air Force

Robin's reflections on money are something every teenager and college student should hear and every parent or mentor should provide. *A Gift for Life* is refreshingly enthusiastic, even exuberant. Motivation, skill development, values, authenticity, competitiveness, a sense of duty and obligation: wonderful threads through these ten chapters.

Michael Kyle
Vice President Enrollment and College Relations
St. Olaf College, Northfield, Minnesota

— A —
GIFT
FOR
LIFE

Table of Contents

Dedication

This book is dedicated to my Dad and Mom, who have been at all the important events in my life and taught me how to be a badass networker and visionary!

Also, to my amazing husband Charlie, and our three awesome young adult children: Oliver, Lydia, and Dorrit, who are there for me every day with unwavering support and love.

Foreword

MICHAEL KYLE

Vice President Enrollment and College Relations
St. Olaf College, Minnesota

R obin draws you in with exuberance, reflection, disclosure, and counsel. It could be with a motivational speech, a journal, a set of notes that you would write to a grandparent, a parent or a child over the course of time, and a diary, all wrapped neatly into ten chapters.

She reflects on her own life, but has the gift of making it seem like you are, in fact, reflecting on your life because you can see your story in hers, your hopes in hers, your aspirations in hers. Through it all, she lifts up four "cohorts" — what she calls "powers": names and networking, money, dreams, and adventures. If you're a cynic about such thematics, you're comforted and amazed at the zest for human interaction Robin's life reflects. It's hard in an age of such economic inequality to think about money and the power that it has over us, enabling choices and decisions and, for many, limiting or eliminating such choices. All of that said, Robin's reflections on money are something every teenager and college student should hear and every parent or mentor should provide. Money doesn't define who you are or even how you live, but it does give you the opportunity to bring spending, sharing, and saving into alignment with a refreshing set of values.

Her own adventuresome spirit reveals itself throughout as she reflects on her experiences and those of her family. Robin's words about her parents are heartening, inspiring, and, yes, disclosing, as she shares painful memories of her father's final days.

The section on names and networking is a call to put down the iPhone, step away from the computer and CALL, WRITE, SHAKE HANDS, SEND A NOTE, ACKNOWLEDGE GOOD DEEDS AND CONTRIBUTIONS. Indeed, it makes you think back to early mentors on manners and being a good person — often a parent or grandparent.

It is refreshingly enthusiastic, even exuberant. Motivation, skill development, values, authenticity, competitiveness, a sense of duty and obligation: wonderful threads through these ten chapters.

We all want to learn from others and find ways to translate advice and wisdom to our own unique experiences. Get ready for lots of enthusiasm, reflection, and love for this one precious life that we have.

Michael Kyle
Vice President Enrollment and College Relations
St. Olaf College, Northfield, Minnesota

"Do it now!"

— *BK* —

Chapter One

NAME POWER

Chapter One

NAME POWER

Mastering the skill of remembering names is the greatest superpower you can learn! Congratulations on choosing to learn and master this important power and three other power skills by reading this book. A person's name is the most important word to them. I'm sure you can think of a time when someone remembered your name from a brief introduction. You felt like a million bucks, right? You felt important enough for them to remember YOUR name! That person's skill (gift) of remembering your name created a high level of trust that will quickly develop into a relationship with that person.

When my twin brother, Todd, and I graduated from Craig High School in Janesville, Wisconsin, my dad gave us the most unusual gift — one that has become a key to my success and is the source of the name of this book: *A Gift for Life.* I'm sure you are wondering what that gift could be. Well, it wasn't a set of car keys, nor was it money, nor was it a plane ticket. It was a ticket to a weekend seminar on "How to Remember Names!" At that time neither Todd nor I were very excited with the gift, but it has become a gift I use every day! Talk about a gift that "pays it forward!" Thank you, Dad, for one of the BEST GIFTS EVER!

It wasn't until after I graduated from college that I put Dad's gift to use. I lived in Chicago and worked as a sales manager at a ritzy downtown hotel. Being new to the city, I knew it was important to start meeting people. Within a few weeks of my move to Chicago, I was invited to be a guest at a high energy networking group called The Young Executives Club. There were two requirements to join: to be employed and to be under 40 years old. Fortunately, I met both requirements! (This group fine-tuned my networking skills that I'll share in the next section.) What I noticed immediately when I entered the buzzing ballroom where the Young Executives Club luncheon was meeting, was how well everyone knew each other and everyone's names. As a first timer, I was happy to see that everyone had a name tag with their first and last names and the name of the company where they worked. I immediately knew that Dad's High School Graduation gift was going to be put to good use.

I quickly recalled the top five lessons I learned from the "How to Remember Names" seminar and put them into action. I put my name tag on my right side so that when I shook hands with someone, their eyes would see my name tag. A firm, confident handshake with good eye contact was important. My Dad would practice this with Todd and me frequently until we delivered a great handshake. To this day, I have people compliment me on my firm handshake. While shaking hands, I would say, "Hi, my name is Robin Eisenbeis" while looking into their eyes. Most would respond with "Hi, my name is (Bob Kimball)." Let's imagine that they do say their name. Immediately repeat it: "Bob ... it's a pleasure to meet you." And think of an association with their name. For example, Bob Kimball tells me he is a builder, so I immediately think *Bob the Builder.* If someone says her name is Nancy, I would think Nancy, just like my mom's name. Try to use the person's name a few times during the conversation and when you leave, say, "Bob, it was great to meet you. I will call you to set up a coffee" — or follow through with a promise you made during your conversation.

Recently, my husband and I sold the home in which we raised our family and moved to a cool downtown Durham apartment with about 200 new people to meet. Pure excitement for me! The first month in our new place, I was invited to a neighbor's home for a glass of wine. At one point during the evening, one of the ladies commented on how I was so good at remembering names and already knew so many people. I told her that it is a life skill I have mastered. They were fascinated, asking me how I remember names. I said that while asking people their names, I also ask where they are from, or a favorite hobby and think of something that matches their names. That night, one of the new neighbors I met was named Virginia. I immediately pictured a Virginia license plate while looking at her face. I also have a piece of paper I carry with me to write down their names, name association, what floor they live on, where they are from and if they have a dog, their pet's name. This helps tremendously because I can pull the paper out of my purse and refresh my memory, especially if I know I will be seeing them again. Having the skill to greet a new person with her name when you see her the second time makes the recipient feel so important, and trust is quickly built.

This summer my husband and I went fishing with a local bass guide on the lake where we have a vacation home. Our guide introduced himself as JT. Being curious and also helping with my name association, I asked him if "JT" was a family name and he shared the coolest story about how T stands for Tucker, the same name as his dad's boss, who was a great mentor in his life. So that is how his name, "Junior Tucker or JT" came to be. For the name association tool, JT is a fishing guide and tackle is very important, so JT (Just Tackle) was what came to my mind. Easy, right? When adding contacts to my phone, I also add the name association to remind me of who they are, and any additional notes about where they are from, kids' and dogs' names, and occupation. For example, if I want to give JT's name to a friend who wants to go bass fishing on our lake, I can just search my contacts for fish or guide or bass or JT. This system helps me become a very effective connector of people and a master at remembering names.

We have a beautiful open sixth-floor space in our building overlooking downtown Durham where I like to write. One morning, a gentleman walked in and I said hello and asked if he was new in the building. He explained that he just moved in so I introduced myself and asked his name and what floor he lived on. He said, "Walker, and I live on the 5th floor." Immediately I thought, *"Walker, walked up from the 5th floor"* and said, "Great to meet you, Walker!" About two months later, Walker and I bumped into each other again, and I said, "Hey, Walker, nice to see you again!" He was totally shocked that I remembered his name and asked for my name again. People love to be remembered, and even more when you remember their names!

There is a new brewery on the first floor of the

building where we live in downtown Durham, North Carolina. A few months ago, we met one of the bartenders, Nathan. I introduced myself to him and introduced Nathan to the neighbors who were with me: Pam, Kyle, Charlie, and Virginia. I was so impressed when he quickly repeated each of our names! I knew Nathan was someone I would need to interview for this book, especially when we returned a few weeks later (without Virginia) and not only did he remember each of our names but asked, "Where's Virginia?!" I told Nathan about the book I was writing to help people remember names and learn other life skills and asked him how he remembered our names. He explained that when we told him we lived in the building, he assumed we would be regulars, so it would be important to remember our names — and he liked that I challenged him to remember our names. Nathan said that after work the night he met us, he went home and practiced our names. He remembered mine because his best friend's mom's name was also Robin. He remembered Virginia by associating her with the cigarette brand, Virginia Slims (perfect association, as Virginia is slim). Even more impressive, several weeks later, I saw Nathan on the sidewalk outside of where we met, and without a second of hesitation he said, "Hi, Robin!"

When I interviewed Nathan for this book, he

told me that his superpower is connecting with people. He shared that he is from a small town/village (Monroeville, Ohio), population 1,300 people with just 62 people in his high school graduating class. He shared that he knew everyone's name in his class —not only their first, but middle and last names AND their birthdays!! He loved seeing how special his name recognition made them feel. When Nathan was a senior, he decided he wanted to attend a large university and chose Ohio University (26,000 students.) Even though his classes were big, Nathan would get to know EVERY-ONE'S names in each of his classes! He also worked at a gas/convenience station in the center of the University. There he also learned everyone's names and made so many friends because of this interest in others. Nathan shared that asking and remembering people's names has become a HABIT— and an easy way to get your foot in the door and excel in business.

I asked him for advice for my readers, especially those who believe they are terrible at remembering names. He said to take small steps. Start with one name and once they experience how happy it makes people feel and how important they feel when their names are remembered, the reward will become a chain reaction. He added, don't feel bad if you forget a name —- just ask again and focus on active listening.

Nathan also said he uses name association. When we were at the Glass Jug Brewery, and Nathan asked for my middle name, (Kimball), he immediately thought of Kimball, a small town near where he grew up and he also saw a KIMBALL sign on a building on his way to work. He said that he practices by repeating names while doing tasks at home. Another habit he has is that at the end of the day, he will run through a list of names of the new people he met. He will also think about names of people he hasn't seen in a while. Nathan is genuinely interested in people and their families. For example, Kyle's real name is Jeff and Dave likes to be called Dave, not David. Names matter. Practicing these simple skills and mastering names will ROCK YOUR WORLD!

I asked Nathan about the success he has experienced because of his skill/gift/superpower of remembering names and he quickly responded: "HAPPINESS!!" He explained that he has friends everywhere he travels. Relationships are very important to him, and he keeps in touch with others by sending quick periodic texts… "Thinking of you because," or "Happy birthday, friend." Taking a few minutes each day to send a text to someone you haven't seen recently will make a difference in their life.

Nathan is the youngest employee (26 years old) at the Glass Jug Brewery and has been promoted very quickly. He attributes his "people skills" as the key to his quick promotions. He said that "a name is an opportunity" — and because he remembered my name about a year ago, we formed a friendship and now I am including him in this book. Making the effort to listen and remember someone's name will build trust and might just create a friendship or business opportunity. Nathan knows his superpower is to connect with people and he has so much fun doing it. He loves asking people about their hobbies because that opens great dialogue and similar interests. He added that by asking a co-worker about her hobbies, he learned she loves to rock climb. So does Nathan and they frequently now meet at the climbing gym to belay each other. At the end of our interview, Nathan described my book as a "survival guide for graduates" and I would agree.

When you start to focus on name recalling and asking questions with new people you meet, it not only becomes a game but it's so fun and rewarding. Here is a nifty example that happened with a new neighbor. I was working in the community space in our apartment building when I met Emily. I asked her about her name, and she shared her Instagram name, Emily Mae DeYoung Gartland. She explained that her middle name, Mae, sounded too southern, so she went to the courthouse and added her mom and grandmother's maiden name:

DeYoung. Now her full name is Emily Mae Deyoung Gartland. We talked about her passions, cooking, and eating healthy food. Coincidentally, that evening I was hosting a virtual cooking class, so I invited her to our spring roll workshop. If we hadn't had started a conversation, I never would have known about her passions, like mine. We talked about rock climbing, running, moon cycles, favorite vineyards, travel, and life goals. The conversation just rolled from one topic to the next and a new relationship was quickly built. After we said our farewells, I followed up texting her information I told her I would get for her. I also made notes in the contact section of my phone about her passions and name associations, repeating her name in my head a few times to reinforce it. Before we left, Emily told me that when she walked into the community space to do her morning writing, her energy wasn't great, and she thanked me for helping her to change it. That's the greatest compliment!

I treated our daughter, Lydia, for her 22nd birthday to a spa day at our favorite hotel in Cary, North Carolina, The Umstead Hotel. Our server introduced himself as Shawn. I asked him if he was a new employee because I hadn't seen him before and he said no that he had been an employee there for two years. I guess our paths just hadn't yet crossed. We talked about how he knew we hadn't met because he always tries to learn his customer's names by recalling or relating a story: such as, they shared a 50th Anniversary dinner, etc. I asked him how he learned this skill and he said all employees at their 5-star hotel are required to go through The Forbes Travel Guide 5-star program. I will add that the bellmen at this hotel are amazing at remembering names and it always makes me feel so good when I arrive, even if it's been a few months — and they say, "welcome back, Mrs. Eisenbeis!"

I investigated the Forbes Travel Guide and saw so many amazing 5-star stories, but the one that really stood out was about Bruce Wong, Restaurant Employee of the year at a Hongkong Hotel. Bruce Wong was known for going the extra mile when it comes to taking care of guests. He once was conversing with a guest, who lamented that his favorite breakfast, honeydew melon juice and yam congee, an Asian rice porridge, was difficult to find. Bruce took it upon himself the following morning to depart early for work to purchase the items and arrange for them to be delivered to the guest's room!! That is truly 5-star service!

What's in a name? I talked with my high school Swim Coach, Sam Loizzo, and was so impressed with how many student athletes he has kept in touch with from his 32 years of teaching and coaching. I asked Sam about his gift. He said he always made a point to get to know names because it made the student or athlete feel important, which then made their behavior that much better because they knew Sam cared about them. Sam also loved to come up with nicknames: mine was/is "Bird" because my name is Robin. Other names included Watermelon or Slick. Sam not only knows where his former students live, but their passions, and family life. He even recalls years when they graduated, or when they traveled to a sporting competition —- even the score and who traveled!! That is some serious focus and wow, does that make his former students and athletes feel important!

Listening to Jim House, author of the New York Times bestseller, *Resetology* and former high-school principal, talk about the power of names gives me goosebumps. When he would walk the hallways of his high school, he would greet students at the water cooler by saying their names. Can you imagine how their behavior improved when the principal cared enough about them by using their names?

Our 20-year-old daughter, Dorrit, shared a story that shows our kids are watching all the time. She is a sophomore at The University of North Carolina Chapel Hill where she is a student/athlete and plays on the three-peat National Championship Field Hockey Team. Her coach,

Karen Shelton, knows about winning, having earned nine National Championships in her 40 years as Head Coach for the field hockey team!

My daughter told me her field hockey teammates have complimented her on how she remembers names of new people she meets. She said she is still much better at recognizing faces (that's easier for most people) but she's trying to be more present when she meets someone and hears their name. This skill she is working on everyday will help her tremendously as she continues to build her network for when she graduates from college.

At every UNC field hockey game, home or away, we always have a parent and team tailgate. We have all become family as we travel together during the season. At the University of North Carolina Field Hockey Alumni weekend late September, I reconnected with Lauren Moyer, a former player who currently plays for the United States Women's National Field Hockey Team based in Charlotte. I asked Lauren what she is currently doing, and she shared that because of a connection with Hayden Clay, from the University of North Carolina Chapel Hill Club Field Hockey Team, he helped her connect with his Mom, who is Chief Operations and Technology Officer at the National Headquarters of Bank of America for a marketing position while she plays field hockey. I followed up with Lauren a couple weeks later to ask more about how she learned to network and for additional details on how she made the connection with Bank of America.

Lauren moved to Charlotte in mid-August 2021 for the USA Field Hockey Women's National Team, the same town where Hayden Clay's Mom, Cathy Bessant lives, and is on the list of the most powerful women in banking. Thanks to that brief introduction a few years prior, Lauren felt comfortable sending an email to Cathy letting her know she was looking for a marketing job and immediately heard back from Cathy's assistant for an interview. It also helped that Cathy is on the board of the USA National Field Hockey organization. Lauren is involved in the interview process now. I am so hopeful that she gets the marketing job at the bank in Charlotte.

Lauren continued to share that her mom is from England, and she watched and mirrored how her mom has maintained long distant relationships while living in Pennsylvania. The key, Lauren said, is to check in with people in your network occasionally and remember important days of their lives (birthdays, kids, accomplishments, etc.). Take a minute and think about what hobbies and passions you have. Who do you know who might have similar passions that you can network with about your career, passions, or life goals? When you have a connection, the process of applying for a job can be greatly improved and move along more quickly.

We also spoke about the newly established "FOREVHER" Mentor Group at The University of North Carolina Chapel Hill, created especially for female athletes. Coach Shelton, the UNC Field Hockey Coach, is very involved with this program and encourages her players to be active as well. Lauren was very excited about this networking/mentor group for alums and current students, something that was needed after graduation. Lauren shared that after she graduated, she was worried about expressing her goals to be an Olympian because what if she fails? But then she realized the importance of telling people and letting everyone know of your goals. Lauren's advice is to be outspoken about your goals.

Mastering the superpower of remembering names will quickly help you become a super-class CONNECTOR! Remember Nathan and the Glass Jug Brewery on the first floor of our apartment building? I met the owner, Katie Creesh, in our parking garage and asked her a few questions about when their brewery would be opening. When she said in the next day or two, I asked her if I could give her my cell number so that she could notify me when they get the approval to open it. The next day late in the afternoon, I received a text from Katie that they were opening and quickly sent a text to 10 people in our building for whom I have phone numbers. We had such a great time sampling their amazing beers: they even created a Hazy IPA beer "Foster on the Park," named after our building. What I found so rewarding was that three neighbors came up to me to thank me for planning the night and to tell me what a great connector of people I am!

Hours before our gathering, we were just neighbors who didn't know each other well and after this simple event, everyone became friends and discovered many things in common. This is what I heard from Emily: "Thank you, Robin, for being yourself and connecting people. Tonight, was so lovely and I had so many long and meaningful conversations."

Kyle said, "Robin, you have an amazing gift of connecting people" and Hannah, a nurse from Vermont, said, "Wow, Robin, you are so good at connecting people and remembering everyone's names!" When I told her that I was writing a book about this gift, she said she wanted a signed copy. Connecting is one of my superpowers and what makes me feel like I am making a positive impact. My goal is for YOU to become a super-connector and build special relationships.

So how do I do it? And how can you? Many people are introverts or very shy and feel uncomfortable talking with others. If that's you, here are a few simple tips for when you go to a networking event, party, or meet a new neighbor.

Start by introducing yourself and ask them for their name. Remember to listen intently and repeat their name if it is unusual. Ask them how they spell it, if it's a family name or how their parents chose that name. My goal with each new person I meet is to have answers to this acronym, FORM: Family, Occupation, Recreation, what Matters). Once you've gathered this information, share your practiced signature "about me" and then say, "(Name), I would love to get to know you better. When would you be available to meet for coffee, breakfast, lunch… and then once again say their name. "Great to meet you! I look forward to getting together again." When I attend a networking event, I like to set a goal of meeting three new people to continue to grow my network. After the event is over and you've met your three new friends, take a few moments and on your phone, or on the back of their business card, write down their "FORM" answers and how you are associating their name (i.e., Bob the Builder) and your next plan… coffee, etc. Going an extra step and quickly writing a thank-you note saying that you enjoyed meeting them and are looking forward to your next time together will make a great impression! Being a connector is fun and helps deepen your relationship with everyone you meet. Is there someone you might connect this person with to either help them or another person? By helping others, you both will receive so much!

When we go out for dinner as a family, I always ask the server for his/her name, if they don't introduce themself as they welcome us to the restaurant. It is a simple way to work on your new skill by repeating their name, really listening, and coming up with a name association. The game has moved outside our family, and when friends join us, they enjoy asking 30 minutes into dinner who remembers the server's name. Give it a try! It's always fun and the server appreciates the recognition too!

During a recent phone conversation with our 25-year-old son, Oliver, I was reminded why I decided to write this book, my first book ever. He told me he was excited for my book to be published because he realized he needed help in remembering names. I asked him to explain, and he said that recently he attended his University of North Carolina Chapel Hill's homecoming and about 50 people came up to hug him, saying "Hi, Oliver" and he couldn't quickly recall their names. I loved that he shared this with me because we have all attended a reunion and if there are no name tags, it is really challenging to remember names. For reunions, take some time prior to the gathering and if there is a yearbook (for high school reunions), look through the photos and names and quiz yourself. Make a list of maybe 10-20 people who were your closest friends and practice their names while looking at photos. For college reunions, maybe look on social media to refresh their names in your memory. For company or conventions, look through directories or business cards prior to the event. Even if you can recall only a few, you should feel proud of yourself. And when you see someone who remembers your name and you can't remember theirs, just say, "Please remind me of your name." When they say their name, focus and repeat their name and make that quick association.

If you happen to be an organizer of a reunion, take the time to print out name tags, as they will help everyone recognize people they haven't seen in many years. I was the president of my high-school Class and when we had our 10-year class reunion, a classmate offered to print name tags that included our senior photo and maiden names. What a gift that was because as we know, people's appearances change and to see their photo of how you remember them helps your memory greatly — also good laughs, seeing the trendy hairstyles and clothes from when you were classmates.

Something I hear often, and another reason I am writing this book, is that people can recognize a face but it's the name recall that is challenging. The first step to making this shift is to tell yourself I am a master at remembering names because our brain believes what we tell it. So, when you walk into a room, tell yourself, *I am great at remembering names* and believe it. It's like the student or adult who constantly says, "I am terrible at math." You know what the outcome will be and the same is true with what you tell yourself about remembering names. Become a master at remembering names. Every day, set a goal to learn one new name. Maybe it is your next-door neighbor, or the host at your favorite restaurant, or a co-worker. Start with people you know and say their names when you talk with them, even on the phone. Just get in the habit of saying their name several times in the conversation until it becomes a habit. Take baby steps and keep practicing.

Hopefully you are seeing how simple it can be to master remembering names and the impact remembering names makes with others.

NAME POWER RECAP:

1) When introducing yourself to someone new, focus on their name, repeat their name, and quickly come up with an association to help you remember their name.

2) Look people in the eyes when talking and meeting them.

3) Ask (FORM) questions to learn more about the person: Family, Occupation, Recreation, what Matters.

4) Make notes in your phone under contacts or on their business card about your new friend.

5) Send a follow-up note letting them know how nice it was to meet them and share something that you enjoyed learning about them or connect them with someone who may help them with their goals or passions.

6) Occasionally review names of the people you met during the day and challenge yourself with how many names you can remember.

7) The next time you see that person, confidently say their name, and watch how they light up because YOU REMEMBERED THEIR NAME! They may have forgotten yours because they haven't learned your new superpower, so just kindly remind them of your name.

8) Set a goal of meeting at least one new person every day. It could be your local barista, favorite server at your favorite restaurant, your mail carrier's name. You will see their smiles light up because you made them feel important!

9) Accept the compliment when they respond with "Wow, thank you for remembering my name." Share that it is a skill you are working on every day and if you want, feel free to share the name of this book, A Gift for Life.

10) Tell yourself daily, "I am a master at remembering names," until you believe it. Congratulations on making the world a happier place by becoming a better connector! Our world needs more people like you!

Chapter Two
NETWORKING

Chapter Two

NETWORKING

After I graduated from St. Olaf College in Northfield, Minnesota, I moved to Chicago, Illinois. Fortunately, both my parents were successful entrepreneurs and I was lucky to watch them network. I am really excited to share what I learned from them with you now.

Let's start with you landing your first job! Take a moment to celebrate and reflect on how you got that job. More than likely, it was from a connection through your college career program, or a friend of a friend, or a parent's connection. That's the beauty of networking! When you let others in your circle (and maybe outside your immediate circle) know exactly what type of job you are looking for, the opportunities will be so much greater! Congratulations! Now it's time to step it up and grow your networking circle even bigger.

In the first section, I shared about my amazing Chicago networking group, The Young Executives Club (YEC) where I fine-tuned my networking skills. Typically, there were about 100 young business executives and entrepreneurs at the monthly meeting. The first thirty minutes was a time to meet new guests and reunite with friends, sharing wins and asking for referrals. What was awesome about this networking group is that every month we had amazing leaders in the Chicago community speak to our club. The speakers rotated between a President/CEO like Gordon Sinclair of Crate and Barrel, to Entrepreneurs like Leslie Hindman, owner of Leslie Hindman Auctioneers. Over my years as a YEC member, I held a variety of leadership jobs including Vice President of Programs, Secretary, Membership Director and President. I strongly recommend getting involved on the Board Level as quickly as possible because that is where the networking and trust quickly accelerate. Within a few years of becoming very involved in the club and on the board, I was elected to President of the Young Executives Club, becoming the first female President of this 40-year-old Club. I loved my role as President for many reasons, but the best was that I had the privilege of sitting next to the speakers, so I was able to really get to know them and they got to know me. I was the President when Leslie Hindman was our speaker. I loved her auction-house stories, her energy, and her success! Following our luncheon, I sent her a thank-you note for speaking to our Club. I then followed up with a phone call asking if I could meet with her for an "informational interview." I had been in the hotel sales industry for six years and was starting to explore new options. I was shocked when I called Leslie, and not only did she answer her phone, but she invited me to come over that afternoon to talk with her. It was a great illustration of the benefits of having the opportunity to sit next to her over lunch and really get to know her — she knew my name and that I was eager to succeed. At our luncheon, Leslie saw that as President of the Young Executives Club, I knew everyone, was successful at sales and it helped that I had an Art History and Economics Bachelor of Arts Majors from my college! We talked for two and a half hours during my "interview" about her plans for the Auction House and future goals for the company. After my "informational interview," Leslie offered me the job of Director of Trust and Estates! I couldn't believe that my career change was happening so quickly, all because I followed up and asked to connect again. Leslie observed that I knew the "movers and shakers" in Chicago and was ready to work! The auction-house staff were all young and not afraid of putting in long hours — truly one of my all-time favorite jobs even though many weeks we worked 70-80 hours. Hearing the stories from families about their connections was fascinating and so fun to see a new owner take possession of antiques and be equally as excited!

Leslie and I traveled the country on Southwest Airlines. This was before you could go onto the SWA website and get your boarding number and since we liked to be the first on the plane so that we could sit in the front two rows where the six seats on each side faced each other, we would arrive very early, but the reward was worth it! In the front area of the plane where we liked to sit, we had four new people to talk with during the duration of the flight. My networking skills reached an all-time high with Leslie as my mentor and boss! We traveled two or three times each week meeting with families and Trust & Estate Attorneys to discuss our auction-house services and to learn about new estates to be sold. I LOVED my job working at the Auction House! Within a few months of my starting my job at Leslie Hindman Auctioneers, Leslie asked me if I would help her train for a 5K race. So, we would meet before work by the lakefront and during those early-morning runs, Leslie started to train me to be an Auctioneer! Amazing what opportunities present themselves when you are eager to always be learning! I have had so many unbelievable experiences from the four years I worked at Leslie Hindman Auctioneers; the highlight was being involved in selling an undiscovered Vincent van Gogh painting found in an attic of a Milwaukee, Wisconsin home during an appraisal. That painting sold for $1.2 million! Be open to always meeting new people and learning new opportunities!

So how do you walk into a room of strangers? Before you enter, make sure you are stocked with your business cards. Set a goal of meeting three new people at every networking event. When you walk in and you see someone you already know, avoid the temptation of walking up to them first — remember your goal, to meet three new people. Find someone standing alone, or someone who welcomes you with a smile. Walk up to the person, extend your right hand and with a firm handshake (no bend in your elbow and a tight grip) look into their eyes and introduce yourself. They should respond with their name, but if they don't, ask them for their name and really listen, repeating their name with "It's nice to meet you." While repeating their name, quickly think of an association to their name. Start a conversation (remember to ask FORM questions: Family, Occupation, Recreation, what Matters) and let them know you are new to the club or city and ask them what they like about it. Or ask them to tell you about their work. Or a favorite hobby? Spend a few minutes getting to know this person and since you have a goal of meeting three more people, tell them how much you enjoyed meeting them — use their name — and ask for the best way to follow up with them (cell phone, business card, etc.). Remember to take a few moments when you leave to make notes about each person you met and send them a quick text or handwritten thank-you note. As the saying goes, "The fortune is in the follow-up"!

Many times, it may take six-to-eight connections before someone says yes to your opportunity or product. Therefore, it is so important to have an organized system for follow-up. Set a reminder in your calendar as to when/why you are following up. If they have asked you to be added to your newsletter, be sure to add them. Or maybe you told them you knew someone who might be interested in their business — be sure to send that name to them. Or maybe they love learning, and your business has frequent educational lectures. Add them to the ongoing list (on social media or in your database). Follow up with a note — because they asked to be added, you've done so, and the next event is (date). If you need to have a follow-up conversation, ask when a good time would be for you to call and give them options (Tuesday, March 15th at 9 a.m. or Friday, March 18th at 2 p.m?). Think value-added. What can you share with them that will keep you memorable, front of mind? If you have a product, send them a sample. Or maybe they love to hike and are new to the city. Send them a map marked with your favorite places to hike, and then ask if they want to join you on a group hike this coming Sunday. It is so true that the fortune is in the follow-up and when you stay consistent and do as you say you will, you will gain their respect, trust, and friendship. People do business with people they know, so be that person for them.

One way I like to keep in touch is by sending birthday cards. I have a monthly calendar (no days of the week) where I have all my family and friends' birthdays. At the beginning of each month, I look to see who I will send cards to, call, or invite to lunch or dinner. I also write the date of the passing of the parents of my close friends so I can reach out to them on that day to let them know I am thinking of them or send flowers or a card. Those little touches can make a difference in someone's life. I love finding special cards to send, so whenever I find a store that has unusual cards I stock up for all occasions. Sunday nights are a great time to write cards for the upcoming week.

Sending thank-you letters/notes is a great habit to get into. As you are building your network, you will be invited to social events. Remember to send a handwritten note of thanks — it will show the recipient how much you cared and will make you memorable because you took the time to write a note. Just like birthday cards, keep a box of miscellaneous cards so you can easily write a note.

I hope that since you are still reading, you are excited about stepping up your networking game. Here's something I did recently that you could do if you live in an apartment building or in a neighborhood. Remember that first event I planned at the brewery in my apartment building? My next-door neighbor, Pam Hickock, (who, like me, wants to know our neighbors) and I decided to plan a monthly gathering for people in our building. We set the date and time and asked everyone to bring their favorite appetizer and beverage to share. It's so rewarding to create a loving community with these events, engaging in deep conversations by asking FORM questions (Family, Occupation, Recreation and what Matters). I highly recommend doing this in your neighborhood, either by yourself or as I did, team up with a fun neighbor. Choose a consistent day of the week you can have a monthly gathering. Because many of us travel on the weekends, we picked the first Tuesday of the month so everyone can plan and schedule it. When the night arrives, have fun music playing and as the host, you be the one to welcome everyone and introduce each new guest to the others or at least one other person so they feel welcomed the minute they arrive. As the host, keep an eye on anyone standing alone. If you see that, help them get engaged in a conversation. Also be sure everyone has food and drinks. Having regular/monthly events, people will trust one another, and great relationships will be created. These events also create a loving family community where you live.

At the beginning of the pandemic, I knew I needed to join an online community to meet new people, as we were in lockdown, and I wanted to continue to grow my wellness business. I also knew that as an extrovert, a new community would be fun for my soul. I had been following Sara Blakely, CEO of Spanx, on Instagram. She is married to Jesse Itzler, a crazy endurance runner and a very successful serial entrepreneur. When I first started following Jesse, he was running an event called "Last Man Standing" — a 24-hour running race! I was totally engaged in the race but also started learning more about Jesse and a new group he was starting, called Build Your Life Resume (BYLR) and another, the Big Ass Calendar Club (BACC). BYLR and BACC were exactly what I needed — a BIG visual calendar to plan/play offense or as Jesse explains, plan your family life FIRST and business SECOND. I jumped into both clubs with several zooms per week and started building a network of people with big, scary goals. I found an incredible tribe/community of like-minded, high achieving people. It feels so good to not be alone on an island, because we are all supporting each other on our goals and our daily "vitamins" (including everyday drinking 64 ounces of water, running or walking three miles, connecting with three people, and stretching, etc.). It's so inspiring to learn what others are up to trying new things they've never thought they could accomplish (like me writing a book) and declaring that I will have a first draft by the end of 2021 eight months from when I started my VIP coaching with Jim House, CEO of The Bookcarver and just 10 months from the anniversary of my Dad's passing.) I am taking a moment to celebrate my efforts!

Thinking about your network, I want to challenge you to look at who you are surrounding yourself with? As Tony Robbins often says, "Who you surround yourself with is who you will become," so choose wisely! Who are your five closest friends that you spend the most time with? Are you the smartest in the room, or are you in a room of people doing much greater things with their lives? Be with the second group and you will see massive, life-changing transformations! What goals do you have for the next six months? Three months, monthly, and weekly? Who is holding you accountable to those goals? Take some time now and write down some big scary goals.

The members in our BYLR/BACC group live around the world and fortunately zoom connects us all! As I mentioned, I show up to every call that I'm able to and really participate. I speak up, share my goals and any challenges. About a month after my Dad's passing, I was on a call and shared about my loss and grief. Another member, Amyla Strode, in the zoom room sent me a private message that she also lost her Dad recently and lives in Chapel Hill, a town just 20 minutes from my town of Durham. I invited her to a hike, and we have since become very good friends. I also connected with a member from Singapore, Sylvia McKaige, who I started following on social media after one of our weekly zooms. We had several hobbies in common and I loved how she set badass goals, including hiking the equivalent of Mt. Everest and working on mastering a handstand. I sent her a message and the next day we hopped on zoom to start a friendship that is now going into our second year. She is my accountability partner and I'm hers and because of our commitment to each other we are making great progress on our goals.

Another amazing individual I met in the Build Your Life Resume Group (BYLR) is Jon Samnick, one of the coaches. It was a summer Monday coaching call with Jesse when he mentioned that he had been in second grade with Jon Samnick and David Scheiner (both BYLR Coaches). It was a "2x4" moment as Tim Smith, another BYLR podcast, *Mind Body Soul 365*, member would say (how it feels when a 2x4 piece of wood hits you on the head) and I realized I needed to ask Jon how the reunion happened with Jesse. Jon and I had connected a few months prior during a monthly pushup challenge that our BYLR community was doing: 10 pushups x the day of the month. (For example, on June 2 we would do 20 pushups and on June 30 we would do 300 pushups.) It was an incredible challenge, where I completed 4,650 pushups in the month of June! It was one of those goals that seemed impossible but setting a goal with others keeping each other accountable made it possible and wow, were my arms and core strong! Jon and I were encouraging each other around day 17, so I felt comfortable sending a message directly to him on Facebook during the BYLR coaching call when Jesse shared how they reconnected. Jon and I hopped on zoom a few days later and he explained that they grew up in a generation before social media. So, they lost touch for many years until they both showed up for their 25th high school reunion. They made sure during the reunion to connect with each other on Facebook. During that reunion, Jesse shared that he was launching his first book, *Living with a Seal.* Jon's immediate reaction? "How can I help?" As luck would have it, Jon was very good friends with a top podcaster and asked Jesse if he would like to be on a podcast. Naturally, Jesse responded with a quick YES, and it wasn't until after the podcast interview that Jesse told Jon that it was his first ever podcast. We all need to start somewhere! That simple introduction of being helpful to Jesse at their 25th high school reunion built a renewed trust and relationship after many years since their elementary school days. Now Jon is one of Jesse's Build Your Life Resume's Coaches and hosts his own very successful podcast, *This is Everything.*

When I asked Jon what networking advice he would give to college students, he thought for a few moments and responded, "Be open to connections anywhere you are." College is a very social time and a great time to take advantage of the many connections while being aware of who is in your circle. Be a "good people picker" because when you meet a person, you are also meeting all the people they know. How true! He continued to say, "Be giving to people and be helpful, build the relationship: the foundation, the cement to your brick building."

Shortly after my conversation with Jon Samnick, I heard from Phil Oden, another BYLR member. He just picked up the phone and said, "Hi, my name is Phil Oden, a BYLR member, and Jon Samnick told me I should connect with you." That's the way to network! I quickly learned that Phil is a residential Realtor while studying to be a health/career coach. I asked him how he met Jesse and he explained that Jesse was a speaker a few years ago at a Fortune Builders Realtors Conference. Phil followed Jesse on social media and joined BYLR when it was rolled out. When I shared details of this book, Phil said he wished he would have learned how to network immediately after college. He has been an entrepreneur for four years and when he would attend events his mission was to learn, not network. He admitted that was a big mistake, and his "2x4 moment" was when his real estate market tanked, and he heard from a mentor "YOUR NET-WORK IS YOUR NET WORTH!" He had a stack of business cards but didn't know any of the people and they didn't know him. Moving forward, his advice to everyone is to build relationships at events. We talked about how "FORTUNE IS IN THE FOL-LOW UP" and how Phil now puts that quote into action with everyone he meets. His final message is that he is working on getting his body to function after a car accident in 2006; he says, "If you take care of your mind and fuel your body with good nutrition, you won't get sick."

I love when you happen to be in the right place at the right time! Last week on our weekly BYLR zoom calls, I noticed a beautiful young lady wearing one of the new fluorescent green ALL DAY RUNNING hats. Jesse was calling out everyone's name who was wearing the hat his new business just started promoting and selling, so of course I quickly grabbed mine and put it on for him to mention my name! The final 10 minutes of our monthly calls, Jesse opens up the call for questions and this same beautiful young lady raised her hand and Jesse brought her on. Her name is Lind-sey Fritz and she explained that she was graduating that week from Fordham University in New York. She quickly explained that she wasn't expecting to get accepted into Fordham, despite her being president of her high school class of 120 students, but her acceptance was due to her college essay: "Life is like a pizza." Lindsey explained how she relates to BYLR's mission of creating a life resume focused on life experiences like the New York running challenge of 48 miles in 48-hour challenge she just completed. Lindsey explained that a "pizza mentality" represents all that a resume isn't and her goal in life during and post college is to keep adding toppings and slices to her pizza. Jesse was intrigued!

During my interview with Lindsey, I asked her how as a college student she learned of Build Your Life Resume. She explained that she's always loved crazy athletic challenges and started following David Goggins, a retired United States Navy SEAL and ultramarathon runner, speaker, and author. Through David, she learned about Jesse Itzler and his book *Living with a SEAL* that details his training time when he lived at Jesse's home. If you haven't read this book, I highly recommend you pick up a copy now or listen to the audible. Jesse is the reader and it is so inspiring. Following Jesse on social media, Lindsey became a big fan like thousands of us, supporting all his crazy races like the last man standing endurance race. Lindsey learned about several groups that Jesse started including the ones I'm very involved with: Build Your Life Resume (BYLR), 30 Days of Excellence (30DOE), and The Big Ass Calendar Club (BACC). For a college student, BYLR is expensive, so Lindsey didn't join (yet). Rather she spent her senior year at Fordham creating a BYLR model for the BYLR Next Gen community. Lindsey's plan was to pitch her model to Jesse Itzler of partnering with colleges across the country, creating a mentorship program within BYLR and helping college students learn how to build their own life resumes! How brilliant is this?

Lindsey made the decision to treat herself to the best graduation gift: a membership to BYLR, the week she was graduating. The next night after becoming a member, Lindsey joined her first weekly BYLR zoom and guess what happened? Yes, as I shared above, she raised her hand and Jesse called on her and she had the opportunity to give her Next Gen BYLR pitch — right then to Jesse and the entire community! He loved it and they are connecting in a few weeks. Be bold! Be prepared! And ask! Way to go, Lindsey!

I was inspired looking at Lindsey's Instagram, and I loved a post she made, like the thinking of Jon Samnick about how important it is to choose good friends in college. This is what Lindsey wrote: "How often in life do you get to live one floor or one door away from your best friends? How often in life do you get to make memories like these? Not very often, so cherish them and keep those relationships forever."

When I asked Lindsey for her best tips for college graduates, she confidently shared the following: 1) Don't limit yourself in reaching one goal. Rather, continue to add toppings and slices to your pizza. Be okay with changing paths as what's on the other side may be better than what you were planning. 2) Know your people: are they good people to add toppings to your pizza? If yes, then hold onto them and really appreciate them. Form partnerships with people who can help you in areas that may not be your strength (for example, Jesse Itzler found Amanda McCreight for his marketing). It's amazing what dreams and goals can be achieved when people partner with others who have strengths different than ours.

Oh, and be on the lookout for Lindsey's book she is writing: *Want a Piece of This: A Recipe for Life.*

Another queen of networking from my Young Executives Club years is Barbara Teresko Karstrom. We first met in the early 1990's at a YEC meeting in Chicago. We had so much fun reminiscing about the "old boys' network" when we became the first two females to be elected Board members. I became the first female President and Barbara was the first female Vice President. Barbara's advice to college graduates is to get involved in every club you join. Being involved, not just being a member in a club, teaches you so much about different positions but also introduces and connects you to so many people. We both agree to join groups/clubs that you are passionate about their cause, because you can learn new careers, trends, and people. Try to avoid joining an industry related club like the Traders in Chicago; when the Board of Trade went computerized, every trader lost his or her job, and their network was all people in the same position — looking for work.

Barbara was on the Board for the Special Olympics for 15 years because she was so passionate about their mission of providing year-round sports training in a variety of Olympic-type sports for children and adults with intellectual and physical disabilities. Same with her 10 years as Membership Chair for the Chicago Professional Women's Network because she loved welcoming and launching careers of new women. Barbara lives by Madeleine Albright's famous quote: "There is a special place in hell for women who don't support other women." Who can you help today?

When I asked Barbara several questions for this book, she encouraged college graduates to travel and take the dream job! This time of your life is a great opportunity to explore the country and the world to see where you may want to plant roots.

She continued, "To stay connected, never miss a high school or college reunion." Something that Barbara loves to have college students do is to interview successful professionals and ask these questions:

1) Where did you go to college?

2) What was your major?

3) What are you doing now?

College and advanced degrees are important, but if you are still in school, please stop stressing over what to major in, most professionals change careers many times. I majored in Art History and Economics from St. Olaf College. As I shared, I was fortunate that I was able to combine both bachelor of arts degrees (Economics and Art History) when I worked for Leslie Hindman Auctioneers. However, my years working in the hotel industry and currently in the health and wellness arena are drastically different from what I learned in college studying Economics and Art History. According to the article "Career Change Statistics" published by General Education on March 1, 2020, the average person will change careers five to seven times during their working life. This number is more than the average number of times a student changes majors while in college. Another report, conducted by the Federal Reserve Bank of New York, shows that only 27 percent of college graduates work in a field related to their major. It found that most graduates' outcomes are dispersed widely, among a broad array of careers. I also found a survey from Best Colleges,, conducted through YouGov, that asked how college graduates feel about their choice of major. Despite 82% of respondents reporting that college was a "good financial investment," 61% said they would change their undergraduate studies if they could go back. The most popular reason for wanting to change majors was, "I want to pursue my passion." This suggests that while many college graduates are happy with their decision to get a degree, they may now want something more from their education. Often, majors are decided for economic reasons, rather than a passion for a given subject. This survey also discovered that "only 14% of millennials (ages 24-39) were concerned about their life's passion compared to 34% of adults 40 and older, suggesting that older adults tend to think more about purpose and fulfillment in their careers.

As Barbara said so eloquently, degrees are important because they can further differentiate you, but find what you are passionate about for your career. We can't predict our future, but we can be flexible and adapt, always keeping an open mind to opportunities. At the end of our interview, Barbara said, — and this has been mentioned several times previously but it's so important that I'll write it again— "FIND A MENTOR!" Your parents will always be your mentors, raising you and getting you to where you are now, but you need other mentors with different experiences and connections to help you get to the next level.

Wrapping up this section on Networking, it is important to look deep at who is in your networking circle. Jamie Kern Liam's book, *Believe It* highlights five questions to ask yourself to examine the strength of your circle of five great friends. (Sometimes only two friends are needed):

1) Who inspires me to not take crap from anyone?

2) Who inspires me to be fearless?

3) Who inspires me to speak my truth?

4) Who inspires me to embrace my vulnerability?

5) Who inspires me to be strong and brave?

How does your strong circle of friends look? Can you right now add a friend's name behind each of these questions? Do you need to add to or delete some friends? This strong circle of friends may be composed of some elementary, high school, college, and work friends. You will feel so empowered having this circle to bounce ideas off, to share situations and help you make major life decisions.

The final tip in networking is the importance of writing handwritten thank-you notes. In today's technology world where texting is the norm, taking a few minutes to write a thank-you note to someone you met or who helped you, will set you apart like nothing else. You know what a treat it is to open your mailbox and see a hand-addressed envelope! Set aside 10 minutes at the end of every day or maybe 30 minutes on the weekend to look through your calendar and contacts to see who to write a note of thanks to. Who did you meet at any networking events you attended? Did you meet a new neighbor? Maybe your dentist? Or maybe send a thank-you card to one person every week inside your network; this can be your parents, siblings, or if you are a parent, your own children. To keep this new habit easy, buy a box of notecards or special cards when you run across them in a store. I have a shoebox of notecards for birthdays, thank-you, sympathy, or just thinking of you. I also always have stamps available so there is no excuse to get the card in the mailbox.

NETWORKING RECAP:

1) Confidence: practice walking into a room and meet one new person.

2) Look people in their eyes when talking or meeting them.

3) Firm handshake while looking into their eyes and smiling.

4) Practice how to introduce yourself (name and one thing that's unique to you).

5) Meet three new people every day — make someone's day with a smile or compliment.

6) Get in the habit of writing notes — thank you, birthday, sympathy or thinking of you.

7) Treat others with respect and earn their respect.

8) Importance of follow-up! The fortune is in the follow-up.

9) Learn how to get others to talk about themselves with (FORM questions: Family, Occupation, Recreation, what Matters.

10) What makes you unique? Share that and find the common connections.

MONEY POWER

Chapter Three

MONEY POWER

When my twin brother Todd and I were five years old, my mom took us to our local bank in downtown Janesville, Wisconsin to set up our first savings account. The bank called the program they created for children the "Squirrel Club." With a minimum of $10.00 and an age of five or older, we were able to open our first savings account and start "squirreling away" money. Mom helped us put any cash we received from birthdays into a piggy bank so on our fifth birthday we each took $10.00 and made our initial deposit. We each received a "Squirrel Club" book in which the bank teller hand wrote our deposit and then we got to choose a prize from the "Squirrel Club collection" — pencils, a sticker, or a small toy. Like some companies today with 401K matching programs, this bank matched every dollar when it was deposited! How brilliant of the bank to incentivize young children to start saving. I remember when Todd and I hit $100! That was a lot of money in our savings account and that dollar amount gave us the opportunity to choose from a bigger toy box! Teaching children at a young age how to save is something that needs to happen more often, and is another reason I am writing this book.

I realize now how fortunate my twin brother and I were to have parents who had a vision to help us save for our future. When Todd and I graduated from college, we received $2000 every Christmas for our Roth IRA Retirement Fund. When I started working, I also set up IRA and SEP accounts making annual contributions into both and now have more than $500,000 saved for retirement! This took planning and generous parents and sacrificing contributions each year from my paychecks, but with planning and budgeting you, too, can set this up for yourself — and the benefits for retirement are significant!

Today, I still do the "Squirrel Club" but I've adapted it to fit different needs now. When I started my own health and wellness business 10 years ago, I set up a separate business account from our family account. Let me tell you why and how this all started. When I was 15, I got my first job at a clothing store, *Amelia Ruzzo,* in our local mall. Mom had a very successful real estate business for 40 years and attended many seminars on investing. She was and still is one of my most trusted financial mentors! So back when I was 15 and I received my first paycheck, she helped me set up separate accounts for savings, clothing, and fun. This was the beginning of a lifetime of "bucket accounts."

Let me start by breaking down how I "pay myself first." Every month, I have a predetermined percentage set for each of my 4 categories (Business, Taxes/SEP, Education/Team, Travel Get Away). For example, let's say my monthly check is $10,000. Before I even see that $10,000 in my Business category— my main account for spending — 10% of my monthly check is AUTOMATICALLY transferred into my tax bucket/category; 10% AUTOMATICALLY goes into my education/team account; and 10% AUTOMATICALLY goes into my travel get away account. This automatic transfer can be done easily online with your bank. There are so many advantages to "paying yourself first." When tax season arrives in April, there is no stress because I have already saved the money needed to pay the government. When we plan a vacation, we travel stress free because the money has already been saved and no debt is accumulated while we are adventuring. The beautiful thing about this "pay yourself first" system is that you don't notice what you don't see and it's so rewarding to save/accumulate money without feeling it! As I am in sales, my paycheck varies each month, so rather than adjust it monthly based on my paycheck, I have a set/consistent percentage that goes into each of these four accounts each month. As a couple, we have done the same with our family accounts: food/entertainment, furniture, travel/adventures, clothing, home repairs, miscellaneous, college tuition, savings, and taxes. The joy this creates when it's time to go out for dinner, pay taxes, go on that trip to San Francisco or buy a sofa that you've been looking at without using a credit card is so freeing!

I have taught this "pay yourself first" savings plan to our three children who are now 25, 23, and 20. Their plan has three accounts: spending, savings, and charity. When they each turned five, we set up a savings program like the one my mom helped my brother and I set up with the Squirrel Club. Still to this day, every birthday my mom sends the kids a birthday card with a check and in the comment section she writes half for fun and half for college/savings. Each of their savings' accounts have grown into enough money for a down payment on their first homes!

Lydia, 23, recently completed her master's degree in Public Health from The University of North Carolina Chapel Hill and is living and working in Boston. Now that she is receiving bi-monthly paychecks she is applying the "pay yourself first" plan to build her savings account.

When Lydia gets her paycheck, she automatically transfers 50% to her savings. My recommendation for people to not have to think about transferring money out of your checking and into savings is to automatically transfer 50% (or an amount you can live without) of every paycheck into her savings — have the bank do it online for you! Lydia is very disciplined (and likes to be the one to make the transfer) so this works for her. She is so proud to see her savings account grow so quickly using this plan. Now that she has lived in Boston on her own for a few months and has a good handle on her new expenses living in a big city, I've suggested that she adjust the 50% from her bi-monthly paycheck all into savings and automatically transfer 10% into travel, 10% into fun (clothes, dinners, furniture) and leave the remaining 30% in her savings account.)

I asked Lydia to share some advice to college graduates when they get their first full time job and are living independently. She suggested making a spreadsheet that includes the amount needed for monthly expenses: rent, utilities, groceries, and entertainment. She said it takes about two months to really see how much you spend on groceries and how expensive going out is in your new city. Lydia encourages everyone to get one credit card. She made her decision on what credit card with an online tool to compare benefits and rewards. She picked one with great cash-back options and a low interest rate and a spending cap of $500/month max. She made a commitment to herself to pay off her credit card every month, keeping no balance due. Her rule of thumb for her credit card is she has two "buckets:" groceries and dinner out. She also always keeps her balance below $400/month as that is what she has budgeted and there is a $500 cap.

Lydia also recently started investing in an online savings program called Ellevest with $25/month. Ellevest is an investment tool to grow extra money, built by women, for women, and is easy to navigate. Her plan is to increase that $25 monthly investment for additional savings but it's a great amount to start. Our youngest, Dorrit, a sophomore in college, invests $10/month with Ellevest — again do what you can afford, just start saving.

Another great savings tool is a 401K retirement plan available to all employees 21 or older who have completed at least one year of work with an employer. Some employers enable new employees to join right away so ask your company if they have a 401K plan. Lydia's company has a 401K plan available, not matching yet, but she is contributing 9% of every paycheck into her 401K that is pre-taxed, so she is saving even more. Currently she has more than $15,000 in her bank savings account earning a measly 0.06% from her local bank savings account. Lydia has decided to transfer $6,000 into a Roth IRA (that is the maximum/year) where she can earn 7–10% average return over time, especially for a younger person who has a longer time horizon and risk tolerance and can have access to the money she contributes if she needs it. Sadly, there is data that shows most people don't make that 7-10% average return due to lack of discipline and panicking/greed during down/up markets according to our financial planner, Brian Mathis with Edward Jones. To break it down, $6,000 invested in a bank savings account will earn $360/year. The contrast with a Roth IRA, if you are under 50 and you've just opened a Roth IRA contributing $6,000 each year for 10 years with a 7% interest rate would amass $83,095! Wait another 30 years and the account will grow to more than $500,000! On the other hand, if you elect to keep the same money in a traditional savings account with no interest you would have $3,600 after 10 years instead of $83,095 with a Roth IRA! Like the Name Power, start small and just start "paying yourself first" to begin a savings account. With consistent contributions, your savings account will grow and over time, you will accumulate great wealth.

Make a "Money List" to help decide how much money you need to survive per month, by writing down all your monthly expenses:

- ➤ Rent or house mortgage
- ➤ Insurance
- ➤ Student loans
- ➤ Entertainment
- ➤ Cell phone
- ➤ Train/bus fare
- ➤ Car, parking, gas, oil & repairs
- ➤ Groceries
- ➤ Cable & wi-fi
- ➤ Water & electricity
- ➤ Trash collection

Total up all of the above and subtract from your monthly paycheck. Are you able to put $10/week or $40 monthly (or more) into a savings account? If you have a lot more money after expenses, I want to encourage you to set up "buckets" for travel, fun, entertainment/clothes/furniture and savings. If you work on commission or have your own business, I highly recommend you add an extra bucket for taxes. You will thank me on April 15th.

One of the main reasons for writing this book is to help other college graduates succeed once they receive that first paycheck so that in two weeks that first paycheck isn't depleted to zero cash. The first few month's purchases are endless with a new apartment: bed, sofa, dishes, cable, dinners to meet new friends, car, transportation. Using the "pay yourself first system" allows you to save money without even realizing it. Create a simple budget of your monthly expenses and keep track of your spending for the first few months so that you can decide how much of each paycheck you can automatically transfer into savings.

Credit Cards

Credit cards can be so alluring to college students with the enticement of a free T-shirt or gift when signing up. But what most college students don't look at is the interest rate; they only see there is unlimited spending and a gift. What often happens quickly, is the credit card can seem like "Monopoly" money and swiping it for all charges can add up to a lot of money. Credit-card companies are savvy, showing you the minimum that is owed, after thirty days of charges typically 1-2% of the balance each month. The problem with making the minimum payment is that it keeps you in debt longer and racks up interest charges. It can also put your credit score at risk. To estimate your interest charges, divide your card's annual percentage rate by 12 and multiply it by your average balance. If your card has a 21% APR (annual percentage rate), for example, your monthly interest rate would be 1.75%, or 21% divided by 12. Multiply that by the balance you are carrying into the next month. For example, if you have a balance of $5,000 you would owe about $87 just in interest next month if you only paid the minimum and that carries into the next month, quickly accruing. So, to put more into savings, pay off your credit card in full each month and save yourself from interest charges.

My Mom, Nancy, is now 85 years young and is still actively involved with her finances. She recommends that a financial course be required before couples get married and to stay consistent with ongoing daily financial discussions. My Mom and Dad always had separate accounts and that works for some couples. If you are married and have a joint account, I recommend taking a couple's financial class. My husband Charlie and I took a Dave Ramsey "Financial Peace University" course and 30 years later, still apply his "debt snowball" advice. Quickly explained, the debt snowball method is a debt-reduction strategy where you pay off debt in order of smallest to largest, gaining momentum as you knock out each remaining balance. My hope is that you apply the "pay yourself first plan" so that you never incur debt. Ongoing weekly or sometimes daily money talks are necessary because according to a new survey by Ramsey Solutions, money fights are the second leading cause of divorce, behind infidelity.

My Mom, my financial mentor, also advised Charlie and me to pay extra on our monthly mortgage principal when we bought our first home, a condo in downtown Chicago. This is an option that banks don't often share because the life of your mortgage will be decreased when you do this, resulting in less money owed to the bank on your mortgage. Making just one extra payment toward the principal of your mortgage a year can help take years off the life of your loan. You can also make monthly payments toward your principal (be sure to note that you want the money to be applied to that month's principal). This method reduces the total amount of interest you pay, helping you fast-track your mortgage payoff. I learned with our first mortgage that the first several years of your loan, the bulk of your payment goes toward interest. The amount of interest you pay each month is calculated using your principal balance so as your principal balance decreases, your interest goes down as well. You could potentially save thousands of dollars in interest over the life of your loan by paying down your principal faster.

You may not have children; however, if/when you do, investigate setting up a 529 College savings plan. A 529 plan is an investment account that offers tax benefits when used to pay for qualified education expenses for a designated beneficiary.

You can use a 529 plan to pay for college, K-12 tuition, apprenticeship programs, and student-loan repayments. A 529 savings plan works much like a Roth 401K or Roth IRA by investing your after-tax contributions in mutual funds. Your investment grows on a tax-deferred basis and can be withdrawn tax-free if the money is used to pay for qualified higher education expenses. Most 529 plans have very small or no initial contribution requirements, and there is no requirement to make monthly contributions; however, if you do as my husband and I did and my mom (for our three children), it is a tax-free savings plan that grows quickly because of the compound effect. The sooner you can start investing in a 529 the better as seen with our own children's accounts. Each of our three children received the same amount every year; however, because Dorrit is the youngest her account has accumulated the fastest. My mom deposited $5000 each year in each of their 529 accounts starting in 2011 (Dorrit was 10 years old compared to Lydia 13 and Oliver 15) with a total contribution of $87,500 that grew to $100,000. Now that Dorrit is in her second year of school, the money has declined a little, as tuition has been paid, but that was all money that was saved, tax free. Oliver and Lydia still have 529 programs and even though they have both graduated from college, Lydia used some for her Master's program and both are planning to attend Medical School and the 529 funds can be used. 529 plans are an excellent savings tool.

I hope you can see why saving power is one of my favorite passions! I want everyone to see how simple it can be to save, using advance planning. I have been asked to speak on many stages about the topic of "Building Financial Freedom" where I share some staggering statistics such as 76% of women live paycheck to paycheck, 64% of women have no money in savings, 90% of women have no clue that taxes are the biggest household expense, and on average, women have accumulated 34% less money in retirement accounts than men. I am confident that this generation of women will drastically alter those statistics downward.

Just imagine if you could save $35/week with an average growth rate of 10%. This is the power of compound interest in an account such as a Roth IRA.

1 Year = $1,885
2 Years = $3,967
5 Years = $11,616
10 Years = $30,727
15 Years = $62,171
30 Years = $339,073
40 Years = $948,611

Isn't that incredible to see your $35/week saving investment grow to nearly $1million in 40 years? That is the beauty of saving and earning interest. One simple way to make this $35/week contribution is to automatically have it withdrawn from your account every Monday of each week and deposited into a separate money-market account (Roth IRA) that can earn 10%. Call it your "Million Dollar Fund," then look back at the above chart and see how quickly that money will grow.

I have already mentioned "Ellevest," an online investment tool that makes it very easy to invest that $35/week. Another popular online investment tool many millennials use is called "Acorn." Ellevest was built by women for women with a tagline "easy-to-use investing and career tools to help you turn money from a source of stress to a source of strength." For only $1/month you can get the financial basics: investing, banking, and saving. If you don't feel ready to work with a financial planner (yet) this tool is a great way to start.

My daughter Dorrit met the developer and CEO of Ellevest, Sallie Krawcheck, at a University of North Carolina Chapel Hill Female Athlete FOREV-HER talk recently. Hearing Dorrit's enthusiasm about how she wanted to start investing with Ellevest inspired Lydia and me to do the same. It's simple; you have three options: $1, $5 or $9/month to get your account started. Then you choose the amount you want to invest from your account each month — it could be $5, $300 or more — and Ellevest will invest that money based on your financial goals. They also have many webinars each month to help educate you as you earn.

Acorn is another popular investment online tool with a tagline "Invest spare change, bank smarter, save for retirement and more." "Grow your Oak" is the motto for Acorn where in fewer than five minutes you can set up investment accounts for $3-$5/month! My son, Oliver, has found Acorn to be a great tool as it rounds up spare change and invests it for you. Acorn allows the investor to choose what you're interested in investing in and how aggressive you want to be! Another great tool to save!

So maybe you are more financially savvy or grew up having parents who taught you about saving money. If so, I want to encourage you to start looking for a Financial Planner to help you make your money grow the fastest. We have worked with three different financial planners over the 31 years of our marriage, based on our locations and our goals. We knew each of them personally before trusting our money with them. Take the time to interview, discuss how they get paid, ask for a few referrals and set goals as to how you see your future.

Recently I talked with Patrick Anderson, a sophomore student athlete on the University of

North Carolina Chapel Hill Track/Cross-Country Team. He shared that in seventh grade, he and his best friend started a landscaping business, offering leaf-blowing services to neighbors. The next summer they bought their own equipment and expanded into mowing grass as well as leaf blowing. Their business was growing, so in their junior year of high school they bought a truck and a riding mower and set up an LLC with QuickBooks accounts. They called their business "Two Guys with some Tools." They were busy working spring to fall while managing school and sports. The young entrepreneurs sold their business (tools and accounts to another company) before they started college as they both had selected out-of-state colleges. Their business taught the boys how to have separate bank accounts for personal and business. They also learned that working for yourself has many benefits, including setting your own hours, hiring people you like to work with, the importance of good customer service and when you work more hours you can make more money. They also learned about taxes. They had a family friend who was an accountant, so they bartered their work in exchange for him helping to set up their LLC and explained how to depreciate assets. This early entrepreneurial experience taught Patrick so many valuable business lessons and since then, he has learned about investing from his dad and now owns a variety of stocks and index funds. Find mentors to help you do the same.

I've made many great connections through the BYLR (Build Your Life Resume) Group that was started by Jesse Itzler. When I started writing this book, Dr. Silvia Odorcic a BYLR Toronto, Canada friend asked me about my book and when I shared that saving power was one of the powers I was teaching, she wanted to offer her money story to help others. Silvia and her husband (both physicians) live in Toronto, Canada and have very stark financial paths.

Silvia attended Cornell University for her undergraduate and medical degrees. She accumulated more than $250,000 in debt before she started her residency with a salary that barely covered her monthly rent. So, when she and her husband got married, she had 15 years of debt accumulated. Silvia learned how clever banks are when they gladly offer young medical residents a personal line of credit that she later learned would be very difficult to pay back.

Her husband had absolutely zero debt when he started his residency as he was fortunate to have his parents pay for his undergraduate degree and medical school. Her husband's mom was an accountant, so she taught him how to manage money and how to respect money at a very young age.

Today Silvia is reprogramming her money

mindset, sharing how her parents frequently used the language "money is hard to come by and hard to keep." Focusing on switching the scarcity mindset to one of abundance has taken time, but she feels so much freedom. Her new motto is "money is love and energy."

Another favorite BYLR member who reached out to me to share her money journey is Felice Nussbaum-Dimartino, from Long Island, New York. She shared that she has two siblings (Hillary and Lawrence); Felice is the oldest. Hillary (the middle) is the accountant/saver who is the independent one and never relied on anyone for money, as she was very empowered. Hillary has eight-year-old twins who she is teaching the "bucket system" as I've mentioned: donate/charity, spend and save with their money. Felice's brother is Lawrence. Both Felice and Lawrence (oldest and youngest) have/had money issues. Interesting study on birth order and money saving/spending, as this is a similar pattern with our three kids — the oldest and youngest love to spend money and our middle loves to save. (Left brain = spend vs right brain = save)?

When I asked Felice what she would have liked to know as a college graduate about money is to look at your family's epigenetics: what was the money language spoken at home and what work/money habits were modeled at home? Felice wished she had received more financial education and guidance to put a little money away every month and watch it grow. Felice experienced the highs and lows of money from her 20's to her 50's and now at age 55 she feels empowered to be on top of her finances. Felice's sister Hillary was wired more analytically but Felice works daily on shifting her mindset to taking ownership of her finances and as a single Mom has made a huge difference in how she appreciates and spends money. Felice loves to refer to money as an "energy exchange" — the more you have and give it away, the more it flows back to you. Final words of advice for college graduates are to take ownership and empowerment of your money early, because the earlier you realize the importance of saving, the faster it will grow.

New Year Goal: Become a MILLIONAIRE even if you make $35,000 a year. Want to be a millionaire by 30, 40 or 50? The beauty of being young is that you don't need a lot of money when you have TIME! The math here is simple: Let's say you're a 22-year-old making $35,000/year. If you put 10% of your salary into a 401K, you'll end up with $1.1 million by the time you are 65, according to an online 401K calculator. That assumes a 2% annual raise each year even if your employer contributes nothing to your 401K. Many employers do contribute so be sure to ask as that is free money! Also remember that 10% isn't really 10% as it is going in pre-tax, so the withdrawal won't seem as painful. Automatically transfer money into your 401K from your paycheck so you don't feel it nor see it. Set it up now and you will be so happy in the years to come!

TO WRAP UP THE MONEY POWER:

1) Pay yourself first.

2) Establish a percentage of every paycheck for your buckets: savings, travel, spending, and taxes.

3) Set up an online investing tool or work with a financial planner to start planning for the future now, not later.

4) Find a money mentor to help you stay accountable.

5) Celebrate that you are on your path of staying out of debt!

Chapter Four
DREAM POWER

DREAM POWER

As a young girl, and young businesswoman, I was always dreaming. Always setting goals. Every New Year's Eve, I would reflect on what I wanted for my health, wealth, adventures, relationship, and then marriage. Once we started having children, I added goals for our family and each child. What I realized was that my goals and dreams became more focused on our children and my husband when I made the decision to stay home for 17 years to raise our children. It hit me one day that I was in the shadows, with the light shining on Charlie, Oliver, Lydia and Dorrit. I didn't even notice this until after I decided to start my own business in 2012 (our youngest, Dorrit was 11 years old) and I was feeling tired of being a community volunteer and charity auctioneer. It was also at this time that Charlie's private medical practice closed, and I hadn't earned an income in 17 years. It was a scary time for our family with three children in private school. It was time for me to start financially contributing to our family's income. Once I made that decision, the fire in my belly was lit and I started to dream again: where did we want to travel as a family, how much money could I save in each of my new business accounts (business/personal, taxes, business, and travel). The second year of owning my business, I had saved enough in my tax account every month that paying my entrepreneurial taxes was pain-free when it was time to write the check to the United States Government. Also, I had the same happy experience when we took our family of five to Patagonia, Chile; I was able to use the money I had set aside monthly in my travel account.

In my second year of starting my business, I got out my magazines and had my first Dream/Vision/Manifestation Board planning night with several friends and business partners. The last and only other time I had done a vision board was just after I graduated from college when I met with a career coach. My St. Olaf College degrees were Economics and Art History, and I had no idea what I would do as a professional. At the time, all signs pointed to hospitality and that is what I did for six years in Chicago, and I loved that career: wonderful sales trips, networking, and fun!

The second vision board I created, almost 20 years later, I was drawn to images of adventures and cool trips. This was not surprising because I was dreaming again! I cut these images out to inspire me in all areas of my life (family, finances, travel, business) and glued them onto the poster-board. When the poster board was filled with images and sayings, I hung it in my office so that my vision was always clear.

I'm sure it is obvious that I love to learn, and I take advantage of learning from experts in their field whenever possible. Recently I joined one of my favorite mentors, Loren Lahav, in her annual "Manifestation Workshop." Loren has more than 33 years in personal development, working for the amazing Tony Robbins, and has shared stages and personal discussions with leaders such as Oprah and Barbara Walters. And has written five books while leading a million-dollar business.

Loren's workshop was powerful, and my biggest lesson was "It's just not about the board." She guided us through how to build a foundation for our manifestation/vision board with steps to review the good and bad from the previous year so that mistakes would not be repeated in the new year. We then set clear goals in nine categories including finances, health, and identity. If you are interested in diving deeper, I strongly recommend you sign up for a Manifestation Board Course with Loren Lahav at lorenlahav.com.

Something I also noticed is that I didn't wait till New Year's Eve to write out my "New Year

Resolutions." Rather, I started my online business with The Juice Plus Company in January 2013, and immediately planned how I could achieve my 1st promotion in my company's compensation plan. I was so laser focused and hit a company record achieving that promotion in just 17 days and earned a $250 bonus! Yes, that was my own money and I felt so powerful contributing to our family's income! Just as I shared in the Money Power, it may be a small start, but just start. I then hit the second promotion within the first month and the top position in the company (National Marketing Director) in a quick 3 ½ years, with a $5,000 bonus! The bonus was proof I had a bigger purpose — inspiring healthy and wealthy living around the world!

Our kids were watching me succeed. In fact, our youngest (at that time 12) made me 20 sealed notes/envelopes with handwritten instructions on the envelope "Open when… you reach Qualifying Sales Coordinator, a leadership level in our company", and "Open when you are traveling." I kept these notes with me wherever I went, working hard daily so that I could finally open the last and most exciting note: "Open when you reach NMD" (National Marketing Director — the top position in our company!) I love sharing the story of the magic of the notes, because they sure motivated me to make one more phone call, to share my product to one more person, to have one more event. It was a fun game that we played, how many cards were left to open. As I've said, our kids are always watching, and they love to see us win!

Our son, Oliver, was 18 when I was going for the final position of National Marketing Director. One day he gifted me with a month's worth (one for each day) of motivational index cards. Some were inspiring quotes from famous people, some were written by Oliver encouraging me to keep reaching for my goal, and some were from other family members. These motivational index cards got me out of bed in the morning to see who was inspiring me and what advice they were giving me. I had the cards laminated so that they were permanent. It's been years now since I looked at the cards, but as I am finishing this book, I think it is a perfect time to start using the cards again! Reflecting on my journey to National Marketing Director, I so loved how my family supported me and continues to do so with my new goal of writing this book and other big goals I set.

The proudest day of my new career as a business builder, seventeen years after deciding to stay home to raise our three children, was on a Saturday in October 2016, when I was invited to share my story on stage at our company's Fall Conference in St. Louis, Missouri in front of 8,000 people. I was standing on stage alongside my husband, Charlie, children, Oliver (20), Lydia (18) and Dorrit (15) and my Dad and Mom. Walking out in my shin-length fancy red dress and gold shiny high heels to the music "Live out Loud" by Steven Curtis Chapman, I WAS SO PROUD AND HAPPY!! I did it! I reached my goal that 3½ years prior seemed so big and scary and my family was standing right next to me! My twin brother, Todd, and Jeni, were standing in the audience right in front of the stage, along with my amazing "Team Take Flight." Together we made the goal happen! I had a vision. I took the daily steps. I kept dreaming. I reached my goal!

Speaking of goals, I had to interview our daughter, Dorrit, about when she first decided she wanted to play Division 1 Field Hockey, as her vision has been crystal clear for many years! When Dorrit was in sixth grade, her older sister, Lydia, was playing on the middle-school field hockey team. Dorrit idolized Lydia and decided she wanted to be the manager for her team (sixth graders were only allowed to "manage" a team and could start playing in seventh grade.) They were fortunate to have a coach who really empowered the players. Alysia Tacinelli, also known as Coach T, was a former college field hockey player. We both recall when she pulled Dorrit aside shortly after the season started and said, "You have incredible talent and I believe you could play on a collegiate level!" What a vote of praise for an 11-year-old who was new to the sport! Her strong muscles and quick thinking from her years of rock climbing were a great asset in field hockey! When Dorrit was in ninth grade, she was talking to her high school Field Hockey Coach about her dreams of playing field hockey for a Division 1 college. His response was drastically different from Coach T's several years prior! He could have squashed her dreams when he told her she wasn't good enough and to begin looking at Division 3 schools. That comment in Dorrit's freshman year, fired her up to prove him wrong.

Dorrit was so determined to play Division 1 field hockey that she talked with other D-1 players and asked them about their process and outside coaching. She started manifesting the only way she knew — writing different motivational messages on hot pink sticky notes and placing them everywhere in our home: kitchen, garage, bathroom, car. The underlying theme on all of them was "Actually I Can, D1 Hockey." The repetition in her mind and seeing them all the time helped her believe her vision — until it came true!

Dorrit also acknowledges three other coaches who were instrumental in her success: (Coaches Liz Sanders, Amy Robertson and Grant Fulton). Coaches Liz Sanders and Amy Robertson noticed Dorrit's drive and talent in her freshman year.

Dorrit was so fortunate to be invited to a small training with both coaches at Duke University. Following the session, Coach Liz introduced herself to me and shared that her business included guiding players who want to play field hockey in college! We immediately met with Liz and Amy where they asked Dorrit to make a list ranking the schools where she was interested in playing hockey and a student. I can so clearly recall Dorrit saying, "This is my list, and my top school is The University of North Carolina, Chapel Hill, but it's ranked #1 in the nation!" With a lot of hard work, great grades, and another Coach, Grant Fulton, the Assistant Coach at UNC Chapel Hill who got to know Dorrit over several years when she played club field hockey for his travel team, Carolina All Star Field Hockey (CASFH). Coach Fulton saw "GRIT" in Dorrit and a future for her at UNC Chapel Hill. I still get teary when I remember Dorrit receiving the phone call from head coach, Karen Shelton of the UNC Chapel Hill Field Hockey team offering her a spot on their team! A true dream that happened because Dorrit didn't allow someone else's opinion to change her goals. She wrote on her field hockey stick "PPW: (prove people wrong)" and she lives that daily. Dorrit's freshman year (2020-2021), she had the amazing opportunity to be a part of the team that won the National Championship! In fact, this was their third National Championship in a row (3 Peat) for a total of nine National Championships! Cheers to living your dreams full out!

When I asked Dorrit for advice that she would like to share with my readers, she said, "Don't be afraid to set BIG GOALS! They may seem unrealistic at the time, but with effort and grit, anything is possible!"

Notes from my journal:

Friday, February 5, 2021

The last three days have been like I've been fighting to wake up from a bad dream. Mom called Wednesday morning to tell me that Dad wandered outside the night before on the coldest night in Florida, *32 degrees!* She found Dad in the bushes and put a blanket on him, and Dad said "that sure feels good," as he had two sweatshirts on and no pants. He had dementia and over the past year had become more confused. He must have woken up to go to the bathroom in the middle of the night, was cold and put on another layer on top and got confused and walked out the patio door from their bedroom and tripped on the hose on the back patio hitting his head on a tree and snapping off the branch. Mom immediately called 911 as there was no way she could pull him up. The paramedics immediately cut off Dad's sweatshirts to check his heart and he was not happy because he was wearing his favorite BK Properties and the University of North Carolina #29 (his granddaughter's number) Field Hockey sweat-shirts. Dad was outside all night and had hypo-thermia (a 93-degree body temperature). To add to his misery, the sprinklers were running early in the morning so not only did it freeze, but Dad was also wet. It brings me to tears thinking about him being so cold and wet all night long. Dad was taken by ambulance and transferred immediately to the ICU. I left at 4 a.m. for the hospital, despite Mom insisting that I shouldn't come. Dad was 88 years old and over the past couple of years, had many visits to the Emergency Room, but always came back home. I arrived at the Palm Beach Gardens Hospital by 2:30 p.m. during the pandemic. I was just praying the entire drive from Durham, North Carolina, that I would be able to see Dad. I will be forever grateful that the hospital allowed one visitor/family member into the ICU every day and made an exception for Mom and I to take turns. Outside the hospital, Mom told me that Dad didn't look great. I held his hand from 2:30p.m. to 8:00 p.m., when visiting hours ended. He never opened his eyes that day, but I just kept holding his hand and telling him how much I loved him and that I was with him and how lucky I was to be his daughter. I had no idea at the time that these days would be his final days on this earth. Friday, just 3 days after I arrived, Mom went in for the first shift at 8 a.m. while I had two phones and two computers set up to try to schedule Mom for her COVID-19 vaccine. Ironically, Mom was so happy that she got Dad his vaccine on Monday of this same week at the Veterans Hospital. We had many angels working their magic as I was able to schedule a vaccine appointment for Mom a couple of hours from her home, but we felt very fortunate as appointments were nearly impossible to get in Florida. At 12:30 p.m., I was able to take turns with Mom visiting Dad. I walked into his ICU room and in my typical enthusiastic voice said, "Hi, Dad" and he opened his eyes! This was the first time since he was taken by ambulance to the North Palm Beach Hospital two days prior. Oh, his eyes — ocean blue and so expressive — were filled with thankfulness. Dad was trying to speak but all that came out was garbled gibberish. He looked at me through his expressive eyes and I knew what he was trying to say: "Why are YOU here?" I hadn't seen Dad since June 2020, (eight months prior) when the girls and I flew home to Janesville after Todd called (three months into the pandemic) to let me know if I wanted to see Dad, I should head home to Wisconsin quickly. I am thankful we made that trip because we had such lovely quality time playing his favorite game of Rummikub and Lydia baked him his favorite cherry pie. So, I told Dad (who was restrained, as he had a very fitful second night in the ICU, trying to pull out tubes and get out of bed, struggling, never relaxing his arms), that I had driven from North Carolina to be with him. He peered at me with a confused look, so I continued to tell him he had fallen and was in the hospital with great doctors. Somehow, he was able to say "Janesville?" — his first words since he opened his eyes.

I said, "No you are in North Palm Beach, Florida." Again, he looked at me with a confused "why?" I explained that he and Mom have been in Florida since October, when Todd drove them both in an RV. He was still very confused. I was so happy he was awake, although I know he knew I had been with him the day before, but he couldn't open his eyes nor move his hands. I told him how much I love him and asked if he wanted to talk with Todd. I was shocked that without his hearing aids, he could hear me (and I had a mask on too!) The next day when I shared my 90 minutes with Dad story to the Hospice Doctor, she said this sometimes happens at the end of life — giving me a farewell gift — that miraculously, hearing comes back. I don't think Dad has really been able to hear for the last eight years or so. We called Todd and I had him on speaker phone and Todd got to tell Dad that he and Jeni had just been visiting him and Mom and he said he loved Dad very much. I took full advantage of this precious time as by now I was thinking that this might be the final time for him to hear how much we all love him. Thankfully I was able to FaceTime with my family. I am so happy he got to see and hear how much Charlie, Oliver, Lydia and Dorrit love him. Dad tried saying their names and with his expressive, beautiful eyes, I know he recognized them. After we hung up, Dad kept trying to say Todd and Oliver's names. I so regret not trying to call Mom, but I had no idea that would be his last time alert. Dad became very agitated and clearly said "pull" a few times — he used to say that often when he was sitting down and needed help getting up. Unfortunately, with his wrist restraints, he never relaxed and kept trying to get out of the restraints. His left arm was so swollen with water blisters from the IV. It seemed as if he wanted to sleep, but he looked so uncomfortable on his back, and he never liked to lay on his back ever since his back surgery many years earlier. I asked the nurse if she could move Dad to his side. Within a minute of the nurse adjusting Dad to his side, a sense of peace came over him; he simply fell asleep and never woke up.

The next morning, Saturday, when I was holding his hand, he was moaning. He hadn't eaten in five days (his last meal at home Mom made him his favorite, spaghetti with clams). During these difficult days, I spoke with a few close friends who had recently experienced a family death. One special friend, Bär, my camp counselor, encouraged me to ask the doctors directly, "Is he dying?" They gently explained that since Dad's medical request was DNR (Do Not Resuscitate) that they didn't recommend putting in a stomach feeding tube and have him transferred to a skilled nursing home (with no visitors because of Covid), but instead to follow his wishes of DNR, where he could be transferred upstairs in the hospital to the inpatient hospice unit. Visiting hours were shorter on the Hospice floor but Mom and I could be with Dad together and to see him so comfortable with no pain, no struggling, and very wonderful care. We knew we made the decision he would have wanted. The following day, Sunday at 4 p.m. we said our good-byes. I just knew that he wouldn't make it through the night. I finally shared the answer to his lifelong question that he had been asking since high school about where my friends and I took his El Camino one night and drove 75 miles (yes, he periodically checked the odometer). I also told him how much we will miss him, but that we will be okay — that he built an amazing life for all of us and that we were so grateful. I also told him all his friends were waiting for him in heaven: Dr. Harvey Hortik was ready to make some more super-hot horseradish; Gerry Hedberg was ready with a cocktail; his parents and siblings and so many more. It may have been my imagination, but I felt him squeeze my hand.

Fortunately, Charlie drove from North Carolina and was able to be with Dad for a short time on Sunday to say his good-byes. Sunday night I had a very vivid dream shortly after I went to bed that I was floating peacefully in the middle of the ocean and large gentle waves circled around me and then moved away from me. I knew Dad had passed and at that time the phone rang, and it was the lovely hospice nurse who told Mom that at 1a.m. he took his last breath. Mom and I got dressed and returned to his hospice room to be with Dad, while talking with Todd.

As Jesse Itzler says repeatedly on our BYLR zooms and over social media, make the effort now to spend time with those you really love because we are not guaranteed another day. I share the final days about my Dad's life here on earth to record them for myself and our family because Dad's passion for life never stopped. What's important to know is that Dad's vision for his business and his family's future stayed strong and continued into his 88th year.

In 1958, Dad started his own building business with a loan of $500 from his dentist. Dad started his business with two concrete trucks pouring basements all over his hometown of Janesville, Wisconsin. He had a very unique concrete stamp mold that was his mark for Bob Kimball Incorporated. Fifty years later, we can now look at a basement and know if it was a basement poured by Dad. As his business grew, he started to add real estate and together with Mom, the Realtor, they bought two apartment buildings (Robin Terrace and Todd Enterprise, named after their twins, Todd, and me). His vision became grander, and he started building steel buildings, including large commercial buildings and hotels. They attended a conference in Florida where self-storage units were booming and came home and built his first two self-storage buildings. Today Dad's company now has more than 300 self-storage units. His dream continued with the preservation of old buildings in downtown Janesville where he bought several buildings and renovated them into apartments, condos, and office space. Dad never retired, keeping his dreams vibrant and his mind active. At 87 years young, Dad saw the need for larger storage units, as RVs had become more popular, so he built two more buildings for 75 RV's and boats. To date, every single unit is occupied! Dad's vision was 100% clear!

Dad loved collecting! When we were growing up, he collected Jim Beam bottles — fancy decanters filled with whiskey. He loved the thrill of finding all the bottles in a collection (political parties, World's Fair, trains, animals, etc.) and never opened any of the bottles, to keep their value high. He had several collections going at the same time. He was always searching for John Deere H Model farm implements. When he was in high school, he bought a 1947 John Deere H Tractor and sold it to help pay for college. Years later, he tracked down that tractor and bought it and decided to start a new collection — finding and restoring every implement for that H Model Tractors from 1947. He also loved finding and collecting *National Geographic* Magazines and *Fine Woodworking* magazines. Dad's largest collection started on a business trip when my parents met someone who collected corkscrews. This seemed like a natural collection as they enjoyed fine wine and having a reason to stop into antique shops. His collection grew to a level where he was invited to join a fifty-person club, The International Corkscrew Collection Society. Twice a year they meet to sell/trade and learn about new finds. Each year they host a United States and International location, so Mom and Dad had fun traveling the world while learning and Dad collected. There is one corkscrew Dad was always searching for (and we've now taken over the search). It is called a Blue Ross Pig Corkscrew and the rumor is that there is still one. This hunt kept my Dad, who is known as *BK*, looking everywhere he traveled. After he collected more than 5,000 and it was becoming difficult to find any corkscrews he didn't already have, he added jack-knives and match safes (an ornamental match box, typically sterling silver) to his collections. This passion kept Dad's zest for life alive, and got him out of bed every morning at 4 a.m. The thrill of finding that one corkscrew.

What's *your* passion?

Chapter Five

LIFE CHANGING
DECISIONS

Chapter Five

LIFE CHANGING DECISIONS

It was 2005. Our family moved to Cary, North Carolina from Dublin, Ohio when Charlie took a job as an Oncologist/Hematologist with US Oncology. Oliver was going into the 4th grade; Lydia 2nd grade; and Dorrit was about to turn 4. It was so difficult to leave my awesome friends in Dublin, Ohio where we had raised our kids together for six years; however, I was so excited to start a new chapter of our family life story for two main reasons:

The first was we were getting Charlie back as a husband and father! He/we made the decision to leave his PhD, the research side of his MD/PhD to focus solely on patient care. When our kids were very young (3 under the age of 8), Charlie was working over 120 hours a week and missing out on our kids' sporting and music activities. He would leave the house very early and our morning cheer would be "find the cure, Papa!" I was so proud of his hard work to achieve his PhD (it took him four years in the middle of his Medical Degree with our new baby Oliver). I really wanted to support his passion and goal of finding the cure for cancer… but I also knew that the time when our kids were young and, in the house, would go by so quickly. So, one day, Charlie came home from a long day of research and patient care, and I boldly asked him, "Would you consider leaving your PhD work and focus solely on helping patients?"

I continued to explain my thinking about how he is so patient, compassionate, and kind to his patients, and how he would make a bigger impact seeing patients than spending half of his time in his research lab with mice. After a very long several minutes of thinking, waiting for him to respond, I felt bad for suggesting the idea, but I knew that in 10–15 years if he didn't make a professional change, we would all be sad that he/we missed out on these years together. Charlie finally responded, "So where do you want to move?" He had been a fellow for one year and then Assistant Professor for five years at Ohio State University. Gosh how I love this man and his love and commitment for our family! We've been married for 31 years, and we both have made so many sacrifices for our family, but life is short and that's what we need to do! Neither of us would change one thing!

So, we started dreaming and brainstorming our

new city. We made a list of what our priorities for our family were. Proximity to the outdoors/hiking/nature were at the top, so we listed Colorado as a top choice and Minnesota (close to Charlie's family to help with our kids) and North Carolina where we had just taken a family camping trip through the Blue Ridge Mountains. Charlie started interviewing at several private medical practices and received job offers everywhere he interviewed. We looked back at our priorities and family time freedom was at the top. We wanted Charlie home more, not less, but some of the practices wanted him to take more hospital calls and quickly take over their practices. After much discussion and prayer, we decided on North Carolina, and the town of Cary, where we raised our family for 15 years! Best decision ever! Within three hours we could be hiking in the mountains, two hours to the ocean and 1.5 hours to a lake! Jackpot!

Changing Charlie's career to patient care was also the BEST decision for our family of five. He was able to attend almost every rock climbing, lacrosse, soccer, violin concerts, swimming, field hockey practices and games. We had family dinners together nearly every night. We went to the beach or the mountains often — several times every month because we could. Time freedom is key, and that major decision changed our family's happiness and memories forever. Sometimes big life changes need to happen. Looking back, that scary major decision made our family even more rock solid and happy.

Being a member of the BYLR/BACC community now for almost two years, Coach Jesse Itzler talks often of the importance of playing offense — scheduling and planning out family events *first*. That's what we did over 15 years ago, and we continue to do it. You can never get that time back!

The next BEST decision was buying our Lake Gaston House (aka the NEST) — another *Family First* plan. Our kids (and their friends) want to spend time at the lake, so we all WIN! We found a beautiful home on the water that has space for many —two rooms with bunk beds and beds for 20 guests! It is a perfect home for big field hockey team sleepovers, holidays, and we have had so many visits from families and friends from all over the United States and Europe including Austria, Denmark, and Germany. Dorrit, now a sophomore at the University of North Carolina, has had the opportunity to invite many friends who live far away, to our home for holidays and summer reunions. Memories. Creating family and friend memories!

Our vacation hometown of Littleton, North Carolina, population 568, has a small and very friendly Post Office. On one of my frequent visits,

I met Erwin, a postal worker. I shared with him that I was writing a book about having passions, dreaming, and setting goals. Erwin told me a story about his aunt, who always said, "You are never too old to start dreaming." She was 94 years young when she started college! She told Erwin (and her family) that after giving birth to 21 children (she married her first and only husband at the age of 14) that she still had one dream, and that was to become a Pastor. Four years later, at age 98 years young, Erwin's Aunt graduated from college with a major in Theology. She became a Pastor and lived out her dream until five days before her 100th birthday! ALWAYS DREAM!!

ADVENTURE POWER

Chapter Six

ADVENTURE POWER

One of our favorite family adventures was 3½ years ago, when our family went on a Christmas holiday hiking trip to Patagonia, Chile. We planned this trip through a former Cary Academy student, Carrie Hartsfield MacLean, owner of Adventure Patagonia. Oliver (21), Lydia (19), and Dorrit (16), embarked with a group from The Cary Academy Outdoor Group (led by Gray Rushin, High School Chemistry teacher at Cary Academy) and hiked what is called the "W Trek" along Torres Del Paine, Chile and then five of the group members continued on to complete the "O Circuit," approximately 43 miles in a week on one of the most spectacular treks in the world. They learned that they could complete this very challenging hike, despite each of the Eisenbeis kids getting giardiasis from drinking water with no filters. They had no rest days, so even when they had diarrhea and vomiting, they had to keep hiking. The beauty of this untouched land was incredible. They experienced all four seasons, including snow, rain, wind, and warm sunshine and a week without technology!!

I asked Oliver, our oldest, to share with me two memorable experiences while on their Patagonia hiking adventure. His first memory: Oliver described how nervous the five hikers (including his sisters Lydia and Dorrit), were when they said good-bye to the larger group of 30 hikers from the Cary Academy group. The larger group only set out to hike the front side of the trek and the five remaining would hike the full O trail, including the backside. Anxiety quickly turned into joy as the terrain changed immediately from treacherous rocks to an immense meadow of grassy pasture filled with daisies. Oliver's eyes lit up describing the beautiful turquoise lakes and rich green dense wooded areas. Their new guide, Alejandro, who at first meeting seemed overly chipper and awkward, became one with them and helped to create a trip of a lifetime.

The second memorable experience wasn't as pleasant. It was Christmas morning and a stomach bug had zipped through the tents. Oliver described the Christmas hike, that included crossing the John Gardner Pass, one of the most famous passes across Grey Glacier and also one of the highest points in Torres del Paine. This was the hardest day of hiking: add the diarrhea and vomiting by several of the five and then extreme wind, cold, and snow! They all trekked on because they had no other option. He recalls that the downhill hiking seemed to never end with "just one more mile" called out ahead from Alejandro. Reflecting, Oliver is so proud that despite physical ailments, he was able to finish the O Circuit strong (along with the four others) and still wanted more. More adventures. More challenges. More nature. More remote.

Charlie and I met up with the kids at the end of their trip in the town of Puerto Natales to explore the countryside for a week with the family of kayaking, horseback riding, and hiking. Prior to our reunion, we did an amazing ice hike with a small group, where we experienced a mesmerizing wall of ice, deep blue glacier creeks and icebergs floating deep into the lake. We were handed an ice spike, crampons on our shoes and a helmet. After climbing a steep hill to get to the glacier, we were instructed to use our ice spike and cross over a ravine. I was feeling brave and went first. I took a step and suddenly my feet (with crampons) slid down the slope. Luckily, I caught myself, stopping me from sliding down the entire glacier! Trying new adventures is so good for the soul! I did something I didn't know I could do, and it was really fun and exhilarating! The fresh, crisp air and the turquoise blue water inside the glacier was eye-opening and life changing.

What have you done recently that has changed your life?

Chapter Seven
CAMP

Chapter Seven
CAMP

Every summer since I was 12 years old, I attended the most amazing girls' summer camp in Northern Wisconsin called Camp Manito-wish. When I was 15, I was in cabin LLII (Leadership Lodge II) with seven other campers and a counselor who introduced herself as "Bear" — or that's what I wrote home in a letter to my parents that first night. I later learned the correct spelling is "Bär," which is German for "Barable," like Barbara. I looked up to her and admired her awesome quote/poem book. We would sit in the lounge that adjoined our cabin with the other LLI campers where I would write my favorite poems/quotes from her journal and add them to mine with drawings of flowers, mountains, and canoes. I love picking up that journal and immediately get taken back to the smells of bonfires, the sweet voices of the girls singing Landslide, the trekking with muddy boots on the portages and the bunk bed chats way into the night. This camp was known for their overnight trips (three days to month-long canoe or backpacking trips). I was happiest when I was "on the trail" paddling, watching the loons, hearing their eerie mating calls, fishing, and eating what we caught, drinking directly out of the lake as it was so clear; we could see all the way to the bottom of the lake. Being out in nature on trails and on the water is still to this day where I am most happy. I loved using the stars as our light and waking up to the sound of great horned owls and red-shouldered hawks chattering to each other. I was the camper who always volunteered to portage the canoe from one lake to the next or carry the heaviest grubber (pack) with all the pots and food.

It wasn't until a few years later when I was a freshman at St. Olaf College (I chose St. Olaf in Northfield, MN because that is where Bär attended as a nursing student and the only school that recruited me for swimming) when I learned that Bär was just four years older than I. I had assumed because she was my counselor and so wise, that she was so much older — silly me! My freshman year, I flew to Salt Lake City where Bär was living to go skiing after Christmas. We skied all day and although it was New Year's Eve, I remember around 9 p.m. we put on our lanze flannel long nightgowns. Sipping on wine, hearing the celebrations on the streets below us and watching fireworks, I learned that she was only four years my senior!! That just blew my mind! Our friendship stayed strong and of course I asked my best friend and camp counselor Bär to be my *Best Woman* in our wedding. Charlie and I have been married 31 years now and she is still the first person I call (after talking with Charlie and my mom) for advice, to share exciting news, or to just talk. We still try to see each other a few times each year even though we now live 500 miles apart.

When a camper is around the age of 16, have attended camp for several years, and have experienced the trail, they may receive an invitation to go on a two-week survival trip, "The Pioneer." It is the pinnacle of a camper's experience at Manitowish. Bär and I just assumed that we would be on the same trip; she as the leader and me as the camper. The shock was devastating when she received a letter from the director that she wasn't accepted! She still encouraged me to go, and I did with my best camper friend, also from my LLII cabin, Cindy Read. We had a few days prior to our training in the Leadership Lodge — this was a big trip in the Quetico region of Canada, where we needed to learn how to survive. During the training we were asked to write down our top three favorites and top three least favorites of who we wanted on our two-week canoe expedition. Ironically, and I felt tragically at first, the Camp Leaders tricked us, and they put my top two, bottom two and my least favorite counselor/leader on my trip. I was so mad! I honestly had no idea how I was going to survive with the wild, crazy mean girls for two weeks. But once we got on the water, alone (literally it was just the six of us paddling on the Canadian waters of the Quetico, we all got along. I learned so many lessons about people and how to find goodness in others. Our leader, who was so shy and from the outside very odd and didn't talk much, was the BEST navigator. We were the only Pioneer group who got to do a midnight paddle! It gives me goosebumps reflecting on the night we paddled for about six hours in the pitch dark, guided by our leader and the stars. It was the most serene, peaceful time I have ever experienced. Three aluminum canoes dipping their paddles in and out of the water, loons serenading us, owls, spring peepers and shooting stars and the most magnificent Northern Lights! Our leader won our hearts after that night. When the sun started coming up, we got to our campsite and took a "duff day" and slept in our tent in the daylight, as we were exhausted from paddling through the night. When we were rested, we fished from the rocks with beavers splashing around near us. We caught several Northern Pike and enjoyed them for dinner — the best fish I had ever tasted! Remember the two girls that were on my least favorite list? Well, my heart opened to them on a portage called "Have a Smoke," of all places. They were wild and loud and not really into nature. So, when we got to this "Have a Smoke" portage, they pulled cigars out of the packs! What?! I was the purest high school student — Class President, State Swimmer, the twin who didn't party. But the "party girls" out in the middle of the Quetico where we literally saw no one for two weeks encouraged us to have a puff — it's a tradition to "Have a Smoke" portage. I did, and although it was just one puff, we bonded. Thankfully, I still have a photo of that moment, where we were all sun-kissed, in our bathing suits, hiking boots, braids and embraced on our portage that brought us all together. We bonded, and the remainder of our trip was just amazing.

What I learned in those weeks together is that how people appear on the outside may not be who they are on the inside if you let them shine. The stories we shared, and the friendships that were formed during our two-week canoe adventure make me smile. I learned to be patient, to see what is inside and that even though we have our differences, so much can be learned by accepting those differences. I've lost touch with most of those girls but writing this now makes me want to reconnect. Maybe plan a Pioneer Reunion? As the Camp's motto states: "The Manito-wish Difference ... Out here, Mother Nature isn't just an elemental force. She's your roommate." As one of my favorite camp songs explains, "break out the oars..."

Chapter Eight

BACKPACKING

BACKPACKING

It was Easter, 2018 — Lydia's senior year of High School. We decided to go on a family camping trip for Easter, about a three-hour drive from Cary, North Carolina. Our family loves to hike and tent-camp. We hiked in about a mile with our packs, food, and tents and found a great campsite, very secluded. We dropped our packs and went exploring to search for the wild horses, famous in this area of Virginia, called Grayson Highlands. We found a cluster of the wild horses and the most beautiful views of Virginia. There were many trails with stepping boulders and while we were walking down one with very large boulders (no pack on my back and no walking stick; Charlie and the girls were in front of me, Oliver was walking behind me), I was chatting with Oliver and asked him how to gain speed while hiking as I'm always at the back of the Cary Academy Outdoor Club pack. He said, "You just pick up your feet at a faster pace" and my response was "I'm worried about tripping." BAM!! The universe heard my fear and I fell forward, hitting my head on a boulder and immediately was concerned that I had a concussion and a second later I landed directly on my elbow. It was the most excruciating pain I had ever experienced. I laid on the hard, huge boulder, afraid to move. Oliver called the crew ahead and they all gathered around me. I had no idea how injured I was. My elbow was bloody, and I couldn't move my arm. They all helped me to my feet, and we slowly walked to our campsite. Everyone else set up the tents and I just watched them in pain. Charlie asked if we should leave camp and drive to an Emergency Room, but it was Easter weekend and we had come so far, and I so wanted for us to enjoy the weekend in the mountains with the family. I did not sleep one wink in our tent that night. I was in so much pain. The next morning, Charlie made the decision that we should pack out and head to an Emergency Room, but first Lydia, Oliver and Charlie (and Fender, our Soft-Coated-Wheaten Terrier) wanted to hike to the highest point in Virginia (the one goal we had in addition to seeing the wild horses). It was a three-mile round trip and when they came back, they were carrying Fender! Another injured Eisenbeis — he tore his soft black pads on the rough boulders. This was a tough camping trip for us (oh, and Dorrit had an injured Achilles heel so she hung back with me so that she could play in an upcoming Field Hockey tournament). Sunday, Easter morning, Charlie drove me to urgent care at Raleigh Orthopaedic where they took an X-ray showing a shattered elbow. They put me in a sling as there's not much that can be done with a shattered elbow. The next day I was in so much pain that I returned to the clinic, and they gave me a hard case to protect my elbow, as I was flying to California the next morning. I clearly remember the look on Charlie's face when he challenged me on whether we should fly to Pelican Hill, California, for my company's Leadership Trip that I won when I reached the top level in our company, National Marketing Director, — a trip of a lifetime, all expenses paid at the best golf resort in the Country. I wasn't about to miss it! So, they gave me some pain medication and off we went to the airport the next day for five days (Pelican Hill and then San Diego for our company's conference). I honestly don't remember much about those five days — just thankful for photos. We left the conference a day early, flying home to North Carolina, because I was still in so much pain with no sleep and being around 8,000 loving people who wanted to hug was just too much! When I returned, the doctor suggested getting an MRI. I went by myself, thinking no big deal. Oh, was I wrong! I've delivered three babies and have never experienced so much pain as when the technician straightened my arm in the MRI machine that had been locked in a bent position for eight days. I thought I was going to die!! I was lying there in the machine, alone in the room with lots of noise in the machine. About five minutes in, the technician's voice came over an intercom asking how I was doing. I was crying asking if she was sure I had to keep my elbow/arm straight and she said yes. I then asked her how long I had to stay in that position and when she said forty-five minutes, I truly thought, no way! Somehow, I did it and walked out to my car (alone) and sobbed. I called Charlie and he came and picked me up as I was not able to drive. When I got home, I received a phone call from my friend's husband, the radiologist who read my MRI film. He explained that I had a TORN TRICEP TENDON and needed surgery ASAP! He continued that if I would have waited two more days, it would have been too late to do the repair. So thankfully, Dr. Harrison Tuttle was able to schedule my surgery for the next morning. Sadly, the day of my surgery, we had all planned to fly to Wisconsin to celebrate my Dad's induction to the Janesville Historical Society Honor. The kids and Charlie still went, and my amazing camp counselor Bär drove from Jacksonville, Florida to stay with me for the two days while they were in Wisconsin, administering my medicine while I tried to stay comfortable in the recliner that she insisted I rent. It was the best decision, as I could sleep in that recliner too. The process of healing was humbling. One time Dorrit took me to my Physical Therapy appointment, and she said watching me work on bending my elbow another 1% was worse than watching paint drive. About six months later I was able to bend my elbow 90 degrees and soon after I was running and relearning how to strengthen my arm with pushups and weights. Thankfully today, I have fully regained all movement in that arm and a few months ago completed a 35-minute plank — another BYLR challenge that included one minute extra per day in the month of July for a total of 7 hours and 50 minutes of planking!!

Chapter Nine
SOAR

Chapter Nine

SOAR

My mom must have set me up to have a passion for birds when she chose *ROBIN* as my name. As a young girl, growing up in Janesville, Wisconsin, I often found myself exploring nature in the greenbelt, an area of nature preserves below my childhood home. I remember this one very large tree just down the hill that was filled with hundreds of migrating Monarch butterflies! It was a vision I will never forget — the green tree that was suddenly orange! One time while exploring the greenbelt, looking at flowers, frogs, and the creek, I must have come too close to a Red Winged Blackbird's nest and this bird went on attack and chased me up our steep hill into our garage! If you've ever heard a red winged blackbird attack call (screech) you will understand that as an eight-year-old, that bird scared me. She kept dive- bombing at my head, flicking her wings and coming very close and then flying away. She never hit me, but I never ventured that close to the tree again!

When we moved to Dublin, Ohio in 2000, I saw my first Eastern Bluebird. I was mesmerized!

I later read in a local magazine about Darlene Sillick, the Master of Bluebirds in Ohio, who beautifully described the bluebirds as a bird who wears the sky on their back and the earth on their bellies. The males are striking in their bright feather plumage and the females are more subdued in their colors, to keep them protected/camouflaged from predators. The article I read about Darlene in a Dublin magazine about her mission to save the bluebirds by building and installing nest boxes provoked a new passion and curiosity. I emailed her many times about my interest in helping her monitor the boxes, but no response — she also had a full-time job and the bluebird work was all volunteer. As luck would have it, I read in our local newspaper that Darlene was speaking to a local birding group at a nearby library. I gathered our kids and we set out to listen to Darlene speak. I was fascinated by her knowledge! After her talk, I walked up with all three kids in tow, and introduced myself. She recognized my name from my many emails and apologized for not responding but continued to say that she had a perfect 20-box trail of nest boxes she wanted to give to me to monitor! This was a dream come true! The beauty was that it was also close enough to our home that we could bike to the trail (our baby Dorrit in the carrier on the back of my bike). Darlene met us out on the trail for the first time and showed us how to keep a log and record every week what we saw in the numbered boxes. We quickly learned how to identify the nests: bluebirds used only pine straw and laid blue eggs; tree swallows also used pine straw but lined their nest with soft white feathers from chicks; chickadees used green moss for their nest with dog fur or dryer lint for the cup and laid soft brown/white eggs and the bully of the songbirds is the European House Sparrow, who made a very messy nest with leaves and pieces of trash. Our job as trail monitors was to protect the songbirds from the non-native European House Sparrows that were brought over to the United States from a man who wanted a representative of every bird that Shakespeare mentioned in his plays. Unfortunately, European House Sparrows destroy eggs, babies and adults who are occupying nest boxes that they want (and these birds can nest anywhere, not needing a nest box like songbirds). They can often be found in the letters of outdoor signs. It was always a happy trail visit when we found nests and eggs undestroyed and thriving baby chicks or the start of a new songbird nest. We would carefully take out the babies and inspect them for any mites that can damage and eat the babies. The kids and I would take careful notes of how many eggs, what type of bird, how many chicks hatched and how old the babies are. Their age can be identified by looking at their feathers and if their eyes are open. It was an amazing experience that the kids and their friends and I had for the five years we lived in Dublin. We loved helping friends all over the area put up nest boxes in their yards and watch their excitement when a pair of bluebirds would choose their nest box to raise a family! The quote in the film, *Field of Dreams,* "if you build it, they will come" is so true when a nest box is put into a family's backyard.

The Rookery

Out in nature, you never know what you will experience. This summer, we took our wake boat, "The Green Machine," for some sunset photos with a drone and we got to witness a Great Blue Heron fly into the trees on "our island" by the dam and to our surprise another Great Blue Heron popped up from a nest! Waiting for the sun to set, we watched him fly back and forth several times carrying a fish in his beak. The videographer flew the drone way up above the trees (the drone can fly 400 feet away from the remote) and we were able to see three Great Blue Heron nests, or a "rookery" at the top of the treetops. How cool to witness this cohabitate nesting when we went out to watch the sunset. Always keep your eyes open to what's happening in nature because you never know what you will discover. As I am writing at

The Nest (our lake home), a red-bellied woodpecker is grabbing seeds from our bird feeder by the water and a myriad of other songbirds are flitting around the other feeders and trees. To take time and just watch nature is so therapeutic and important in our high-tech world.

Early this summer when I was writing at the lake, I got to witness another beautiful act of nature, watching a hummingbird. It is so amazing how they can hover, fly backwards, and use their long tongue that wraps around their brain to get nectar from flowers or from a hummingbird feeder. I can't wait for the females to arrive and the "jibber jabber" of the males and females fighting for food. I've added a few additional feeders this year so that hopefully they realize there is enough to go around. If you don't already have bird feeders where you live (even apartment living we get about 20 different species a day), I want to encourage you to visit a local bird store and get started. It's time to SOAR!

Chapter Ten

CLIMB THAT MOUNTAIN

Chapter Ten

CLIMB THAT MOUNTAIN

A sport that took over our family's heart about ten years ago is rock climbing. It all started when a friend from Ohio, Jen Whipple, came to visit our family in Cary, North Carolina on a December weekend. The weather was cold and rainy and as we are all into adventures, she asked if we had ever tried rock climbing. Coincidentally, a good friend of ours, Joel Graybeal, had just opened an indoor climbing gym and invited our family to check it out. We were all "hooked" (pun intended) immediately, but Dorrit found her first true passion and joined the competitive climbing circuit. Oliver and Lydia would drive Dorrit to her team practice, and loved the sport so much that they would climb and subsequently got hired at our local climbing gym, Triangle Rock Club, working the front desk, leading classes and coaching summer camps. The beauty of rock climbing is it's a perfect sport for families as age and strength are independent as each climbs at their ability. We took a family climbing trip to Red Rock in Las

Vegas and climbed 75' boulders as a family! The views from the top were spectacular. Dorrit went on to compete at Nationals when she was in sixth grade, and then discovered field hockey where she is now thriving. Both Oliver and Lydia continue to climb, but Oliver tries to fit in climbing a couple times a week. When I asked him about his preference of indoor vs outdoor climbing, he responded he loves the ease of indoor where he can stop by the gym after work and there is no preparation needed before a climb: harness up and climb. However, he prefers climbing outside as it allows you to disconnect and become relaxed even in a more dangerous environment. He loves being one with nature and enjoys the preparation of gathering all the gear and triple checking holds and safety of the ropes and carabiners. Oliver's favorite part of climbing outdoors is the unparallel sensation of tranquility of being in nature, with no gym music blaring, just the beautiful sounds of the wind and birds and incredible scenery.

Oliver's advice as a 2018 UNC Chapel Hill Graduate is to make time to explore nature. He has found it can be easy to lose track of long-term goals if one purely focuses on day-to-day stresses, however, getting outside greatly helps improves one's mental health and allows him to take the necessary time with no technology distractions, to review the week's accomplishments and celebrate those wins.

Recently, Dorrit and I were driving across a lake in Cary, North Carolina where I monitored a nesting pair of bald eagles about eight years ago for many years. Unfortunately, the pair left the lake several years ago as the lake had an infiltration of chemicals. However, today we saw a BALD EAGLE resting above the lake. I want to look at that eagle as a sign of great times ahead!

When was the last time you went to a children's museum and gardens (with no kids)? I did just that recently at our local Museum of Life and Sciences in Durham, North Carolina and felt like a kid in a candy store!! They have the most beautiful greenhouse with 30-50 different species of tropical butterflies! To just be present and allow the butterflies to fly around me was an incredible experience! I decided to buy a year's membership and Oliver (25) and Dorrit (20) who live nearby are as excited as I am about frequent visits to the Museum. I get the same happy experience when I visit our local art museum. Take advantage of these amazing museums and gardens many of whom have free days for the community!

Throughout this book I have shared many fun exercise challenges. I love short, thirty-day challenges as they are doable and friends like to join me, making it more fun. A new monthly challenge that I started in the New Year of 2022 is to run or walk three miles every day for the entire month.

If you aren't a runner, it may seem like too big of a goal, so I encourage you to just get out and walk and keep track of your daily mileage. I think you will be surprised at how easily you can add three miles to your day. Once you are feeling stronger, try running a mile or two and keep working on adding longer runs/walks until you hit three miles. By the end of the month, my guess is that you will want to continue into the next month and quite possibly (hopefully) you have created a new lifetime habit.

Eating more plants and adding more color to your daily food is also another important goal because we know it to be true, "when you don't have your health, you don't have anything." Another famous quote is "health is not valued till sickness comes." I am so passionate about my desire to live a healthy and long life so that I can hike mountains with our grandchildren and children and spend time in nature, exercising every day and eating a mostly plant diet. Maybe my book has inspired you to do the same, and we will all be on top of that mountain. I hope this book inspires you to master the four powers:

1) Remember Names/Network

2) Money

3) Dream

4) Adventure

I look forward to hearing your success stories of you climbing "your mountains." Climb on!

You can find me on:

FB: Robin Kimball Eisenbeis
IG: @daretodreamwithrobin and
    @daretogrowwithrobin
Email: robin2109@me.com
Phone: 919-306-8145
www.agiftforlifebook.com

THANK YOU

For years, close friends and family have encouraged me to write a book to teach others what comes naturally to me. It wasn't until last year, when I joined the Build Your Life Resume (BYLR) community, led by Jesse Itzler, where I met many others who were writing books. I thought if they can write a book, so can I. When I shared this goal with my Life Coach, Laurie Wintonick, faster than snapping her fingers, Laurie connected me with an amazing book coach and now friend, Jim House, who guided me on how to "get that great book I had inside of my head on to paper". My goal has always been to create a book that my children will be proud of and leave a legacy to each of you readers.

I want to thank each of the legends I interviewed in my book, who openly shared their hearts to each of you. Next, I want to give a whole-hearted and sincere thanks to Brian Thomas, my writing accountability partner. I am so grateful for our partnership, encouragement, and friendship. To Amyla Strode, thank you for our spiritual connection and monthly hikes. Christie Nix, you were the first to say, "I can't wait for you to sign *my* book!" Your support has meant the world to me.

My heart is overflowing with thanks to my wonderful friend and author David Scheiner as he kindly introduced me to key players in the process of finishing my manuscript beginning with the fabulous copy editor, Bill Worth, who is living his dream on the beautiful island of Maui. His attention to detail proved incredibly valuable, especially the encouragement to remove many of my exclamation marks. (Those of you who know me, understand that I always speak with excitement and exclamation marks in my writing). Secondly the introduction to Marty Marsh, my technical layout, page design and cover creator, what would I do without you?! From our first call, I knew we would be lifetime friends! Thank you for listening to my vision and designing a book that represents me.

To my family, especially my Dad and Mom, for always believing I would do great things. To Charlie, thank you for asking me on a date at St. Olaf College — 34 years ago! Every day has been made better because of our love. Thanks for being my best friend, who made all my dreams possible. Where would we be without you? To our three young adult children, Oliver, Lydia, and Dorrit — no mother could be more proud of her kids than I am of you. You continue to inspire me every day.

ROBIN KIMBALL EISENBEIS

Robin Kimball Eisenbeis is the owner of Bluebird Lifestyle Solutions, where she has helped change the health and mindset of thousands and is recognized globally. She practices what she coaches, from 5 a.m. workouts, currently training for two half-marathons and "29029Everesting", where she will climb the equivalent of Mt. Everest, the highest mountain in the world, in 36 hours with her husband, Charlie.

She lives life full-out and holds a personal record of a 35-minute plank and 91 pushups. She is the mother of three happy, healthy, and grounded young adults — two of whom have graduated from The University of North Carolina Chapel Hill, and the youngest is a sophomore student/athlete on the National Championship Field Hockey Team. This book, *A Gift for Life,* shares her four powers to help college graduates soar through life. On social media, you can witness Robin's family adventures, including camping, birding, hiking, planking, wake surfing, and field hockey!

Robin is a professional networker, with a natural ability to ask curious questions that reveal common factors. When Robin arrives, there is not a stranger in the room! Robin is married to Charlie, an Oncologist/Hematologist. The couple lives in Durham, North Carolina.

Find out more about Robin Kimball Eisenbeis:

Instagram: @daretodreamwithrobin and @daretogrowwithrobin
Facebook: Robin Kimball Eisenbeis
Website: www.agiftforlifebook.com

Lightning Source UK Ltd.
Milton Keynes UK
UKHW021955230322
400527UK00008B/313/J

9 798985 589603